D1262992

Fourth Amendment Rights

Fourth Amendment Rights

J. David Hirschel
University of North Carolina

Lexington Books
D.C. Heath and Company
Lexington, Massachusetts
Toronto

792769

Library of Congress Cataloging in Publication Data

Hirschel, J. David.
    Fourth amendment rights.

    Bibliography: p.
    Includes index.
    1. Searches and seizures—United States. I. Title.
KF9630.H57   345'.73'052   78-57161
ISBN 0-669-02361-2

Copyright © 1979 by D.C. Heath and Company

All rights reserved. No part of this publication may be reproduced or transmit-
ted in any form or by any means, electronic or mechanical, including
photocopy, recording, or any information storage or retrieval system, without
permission in writing from the publisher.

Published simultaneously in Canada.

Printed in the United States of America.

International Standard Book Number: 0-669-02361-2

Library of Congress Catalog Card Number: 78-57161

To my love, my wife Fran

Contents

List of Figures

List of Tables

Foreword

This is indeed a welcome study of an important topic in our law governing criminal trials. It is important because it deals both with the citizen's right to be free of unreasonable search and seizure and with the increasing difficulty faced by law enforcement officials seeking to ensure that violators of the law receive swift and sure punishment. It deals with the exclusionary rule, the rule that says that illegally obtained evidence cannot be used against a defendant in a criminal trial.

In pursuing his study, Dr. Hirschel has followed a long academic tradition of providing constructive criticism of our legal system. Busy judges and legislators can recognize and define issues concerning the law that beg for serious investigation, but they cannot themselves carry out that investigation. Similarly, law enforcement officials can draw attention to their impressions of how particular legal rules affect their operations, but seldom have the resources to document those impressions. Regarding this problem area—the dilemma of how to operationalize the Fourth Amendment privilege against unreasonable searches and seizures without depriving citizens unnecessarily of state protection against criminal predators—judges first began asking whether the already available theoretical remedies for unreasonable searches were in fact effective. Those theoretical remedies include civil suit against and criminal prosecution of violating law enforcement officers, internal police review and external civilian review leading to discipline of those officers, and injunctions and special federal actions against both state and federal officials. Scholars responded with well designed research projects that eventually indicated that none of the theoretical remedies were effective. Finally the judges held that because illegal searches could not be prevented, the evidence so obtained would not be admissible in court. Since that holding, the judges have been asking whether the exclusionary rule has been enforced in the lower courts and, if so, what its effect has been. Again the scholars have responded. A considerable literature on the impact of the rule has developed and is cited by Dr. Hirschel, but none of that research has attempted to determine how police, defense, and prosecution officials view it. This book addresses that issue. As such, it adds to the scholarly gloss on the exclusionary rule.

In carrying out this study, Dr. Hirschel demonstrates the utility of the relatively new interdisciplinary research-oriented graduate programs in criminal justice, of which he is a product. Educated first in the law, Dr. Hirschel then spent five years as a doctoral student at the School of Criminal Justice of the State University of New York at Albany. That program integrates the approaches of the basic behavioral and social science disciplines in its eclectic teaching of prospective research personnel for study of crime problems. In this study, that blending of disciplines is quite apparent in both the research design and the implementing methodology. The result is material for a true Brandeis brief for modification of the exclusionary rule. Although the concept of the Brandeis brief—documentation of argument with factual data obtained through research—is widely accepted among lawyers, few have the education in social science research methods to carry it off. Graduates of the new integrated interdisciplinary doctoral programs that are focused on the social problem of crime can provide the necessary documentation.

This study provides new basic information for legislators and judges who might face the question of whether the exclusionary rule should be modified or abandoned. It discusses the extent to which police officers, prosecutors, and defense attorneys agree with courts in their definition of what constitutes reasonableness in a warrantless search. It investigates the impact of whether a given search is productive of incriminatory evidence on the extent of their agreement with what constitutes reasonableness. It also tests whether the exclusionary rule does in fact deter unreasonable searches, whether it appears to discipline police who make unreasonable warrantless searches, and whether, in fact, persons who have been subjected to unreasonable searches should be compensated by having the evidence so obtained excluded at trial. A byproduct of the study is some interesting insight into how well police officers and lawyers (both prosecutors and defense attorneys) understand this area of the law. That information is food for thought by both law school and criminal justice program professors. It is also of some interest to note that fourteen lawyers purported to be familiar with a purely fictional case, but that only one police officer made that claim.

As might be expected when the problem under study is as important as enforcement of the Fourth Amendment to our Constitution, reasonable men differ as to what our future policy should be. It is somewhat surprising to find that, among the principals—police and lawyers—who deal with the exclusionary rule on a day-to-day basis, there is almost no support for its abolition. One possible modification suggested previously in the literature did receive cautious support. There is strong evidence that, should the suggested modification be made, it should be accompanied by new police rules of conduct that are effectively enforced. This of course raises the issues of who should promulgate and enforce such rules. Possible alternatives or supplements to the exclusionary rule are also explored, including award of compensation to the person whose rights are violated.

This book concludes with recommendations for change based on the empirical findings in the study. They are imaginative and reasonable; they merit careful attention and wide debate. Perhaps there are more reasonable possibilities, but a prima facie case has been made for those advanced here. The burden of continuing the dialogue begun in this book would now seem to shift to those who remain unpersuaded.

Richard A. Myren
School of Justice
The American University
Washington, D.C.

Acknowledgments

I wish to express my deep gratitude to the faculty of the School of Criminal Justice at the State University of New York at Albany for the invaluable advice and assistance they provided, and in particular I wish to thank Jack M. Kress, Richard A. Myren, Harold E. Pepinsky, William P. Brown, and Graeme R. Newman.

I would also like to acknowledge my appreciation of the men in the field without whose assistance this study would not have been possible, and especially Dick, George, Joe, and Mick.

Last, but not least, a special word of thanks to my wife Fran for her help and support in the many stages of the project.

1 Introduction

The Fourth Amendment provides that "The right of the people to be secure in their persons, houses, papers, and effects, against unreasonable searches and seizures, shall not be violated. . . ."[1]

Mindful of the abuses English citizens had at earlier times received at the hands of their government, the founding fathers sought to bestow upon private individuals on American soil a guarantee against unreasonable governmental intrusion into their lives. Despite the Fourth Amendment's strong and explicit statement of this guarantee and the detailed instructions it contains for the issuance of warrants,[2] the Fourth Amendment does not indicate how compliance with its provisions is to be ensured. The problem is twofold: first, how to protect the public from unreasonable searches and seizures by deterring governmental officials from making them; and second, when such protection has been insufficient, how to punish the errant official and compensate the wronged individual.

At present there are several means for ensuring the enforcement of Fourth Amendment rights. The criminal law and civil law both contain provisions for that purpose. There are injunctions and special federal actions which can be used against both state and federal officials. There is internal police review and external civilian review. There is, finally, the exclusionary rule, which in terms of the Fourth Amendment requires that evidence seized as the result of an illegal search shall not be admissible in court. Each of these procedures has special advantages and disadvantages. Each is relied on to a different degree and for a different purpose.

A history of the search for a reasonable protection of Fourth Amendment rights evidenced a growing reliance on the exclusionary rule as the primary mode of enforcement as a response to increased disillusionment with other procedures. Today, however, the drawbacks of the exclusionary rule are more apparent and the cry has arisen for its modification or abolition.[3]

This study is exploratory in nature, comprising a somewhat different approach to the problem. Previous research has generally concentrated on examining the frequency with which the various procedures[4] have been used and, in the case of the exclusionary rule, on the nature and disposition of cases in which suppression hearings have been held.[5] Some attitudinal research has explored general feelings about the effects of the exclusionary rule.[6] Other research has examined specific effects.[7] No research, however, has explored the whole general area of search and seizure and attempted to relate differential

1

perceptions of Fourth Amendment problems to an external theoretical framework.

The dicta of judges, the writings of scholars, and the proposals of professional and legislative bodies underscore the significance of the subject as a topic for research. The need for research in the area has also been declared. As stated in 1974 by the Supreme Court in *U.S.* v. *Calandra*, "There is some disagreement as to the practical efficacy of the exclusionary rule, and as the Court noted in *Elkins* v. *U.S.* relevant 'empirical statistics are not available.' "[8] Two years later the Court again emphasized the lack of data.[9]

This study presents a theoretical framework for viewing the problem of protecting Fourth Amendment rights, and examines police, prosecution, and defense perceptions of various facets of the problem within this framework. The objective is to locate and examine areas of conflict and suggest what modifications might be made in the present situation to best ensure the Fourth Amendment's guarantee against unreasonable search and seizure with the least overall cost to the interests of law enforcement.

The theoretical framework of the study is suggested by the Fourth Amendment's division of searches into reasonable and unreasonable searches,[10] and by the exclusionary rule's focus on searches that produce contraband or incriminating evidence. Despite the oft-stated court preference for search by warrant,[11] the vast majority of searches are made without a warrant. Because of the different considerations in searches made with and without warrants, and because of practical constraints in this research, the bulk of the study will focus on warrantless search and seizure. Because of different legal and practical considerations, border, airport and administrative searches were considered outside the ambit of this project.

After surveying reactions to the standard of reasonableness laid down by the courts in selected cases, and investigating the problem of unproductive police searches, the study focuses on attitudes toward and perceptions of, the exclusionary rule and its alternatives. The groundwork for concrete proposals is laid by examining evaluations of the present situation and by gauging the mood for and desired direction of change. The study begins by examining the line drawn by the courts between reasonable and unreasonable searches and compares the reactions of police, defense, and prosecution officials to court decisions in selected cases. It then explores the differential perceptions of the percentage of police searches which uncover neither contraband nor incriminating evidence. By combining these findings, individual and group perspectives on the nature of warrantless search and seizure are developed. Focus is then turned to the positive side of the exclusionary rule, and an evaluation is undertaken of the deterrent, disciplinary, and compensatory functions it performs. Subsequently, the effects of and impediments to proposed modifications of the rule are estimated. The question of who should issue, and who enforce, police rules of conduct in search and seizure is then examined. Finally, the potential of other procedures to provide deterrent, disciplinary, and compensatory functions is explored.

The significance of the first part of the study is that it indicates whether the courts in selected cases most represent the views of police, prosecution, or defense officials in striking a boundary between reasonable and unreasonable searches; it enables the courts to see how others view their decisions and serves as a guide for the courts by indicating what others consider reasonable or unreasonable searches. Finally, it presents perceptions of the law "in action" and gives insight into a police officer's decision to undertake a search.

By providing the different group estimates of the extent to which police searches uncover neither contraband nor incriminating evidence, an indication is given of how large the issue of unproductive police searches appears to be. By presenting individual and group perspectives on warrantless search and seizure, a context is provided for views on protecting Fourth Amendment rights. The development of these perspectives is, indeed, considered to be of great importance in understanding various respondent attitudes toward the exclusionary rule and its alternatives; for it may well be that differences of opinion about the exclusionary rule and its alternatives arise not so much from differential evaluations of their worth as from differential perceptions of the search and seizure situation. Our exploration of the positive side of the exclusionary rule provides differential evaluations of the rule as a deterrent, disciplinary, and compensatory mechanism. By examining reactions to proposed modifications of the exclusionary rule, a gauge is obtained, in advance of legislation or judicial decision, of the sentiments toward, impediments to, and likely effects of these suggested modifications. Finally, by exploring attitudes toward the use of other procedures to protect Fourth Amendment rights, different perceptions are obtained of the potential of these procedures to fulfill functions which have been left to the exclusionary rule.

Each part of this study is thus significant in its own right. As a whole it adds important knowledge to our understanding of the problems of protecting Fourth Amendment rights and suggests, through a combination of empirical research and analytic deduction, a framework that will better ensure the Fourth Amendment's guarantee against unreasonable search and seizure with the least overall cost to the interests of law enforcement.

Notes

1. United States *Constitution,* Amendment 4.

2. United States *Constitution,* Amendment 4 continues: "and no warrants shall issue, but upon probable cause, supported by Oath or affirmation, and particularly describing the place to be searched, and the person or things to be seized."

3. This is evidenced by

(a) Dicta in judicial decisions. See, e.g., (1) *Coolidge* v. *New Hampshire* 403 U.S. 443 (1971): "From the several opinions that have been filed in this case it is apparent that the law of search and seizure is due for an overhauling. . . . I would begin this process of reevaluation by overruling *Mapp* v. *Ohio* 367 U.S. 643 (1961) and *Ker* v. *California* 374 U.S. 23 (1963)." (Harlan, J., concurring at 490); (2) *Bivens* v. *Six Unknown Named Agents of Federal Bureau of Narcotics* 403 U.S. 388 (1971): "In characterizing the suppression doctrine as an anomalous and ineffective mechanism with which to regulate laws and enforcement, I intend no reflection on the motivation of those members of this Court who hoped it would be a means of enforcing the Fourth Amendment. . . . But we can and should be faulted for clinging to an unworkable and irrational concept of law. My criticism is that we have taken so long to find better ways to accomplish these desired objectives. And there are better ways" (Burger, C.J., dissenting at 420); (3) *Stone, Warden* v. *Powell* 428 U.S. 465 (1976): "For reasons stated in my dissent in *Bivens,* it seems clear to me that the exclusionary rule has been operative long enough to demonstrate its flaws. The time has come to modify its reach, even if it is retained for a small and limited category of cases" (Burger, C.J., concurring at 496). "I feel constrained to say, however, that I would join four or more other Justices in substantially limiting the reach of the exclusionary rule as presently administered under the Fourth Amendment in federal and state criminal trials" (White, J., dissenting at 537).

(b) Articles. See, e.g., (1) Harvey Wingo, "Growing Disillusionment with the Exclusionary Rule," *Southwestern Law Journal* 25 (1971):573-593; (2) William J. Cox, "The Decline of the Exclusionary Rule: An Alternative to Injustice," *Southwestern University Law Review* 4 (1972):68-91; (3) Carter LaPrade, "An Alternative to the Exclusionary Rule Presently Administered Under the Fourth Amendment," *Connecticut Bar Journal* 48 (1974):100-110.

(c) Recent judicial and legislative proposals: See, e.g., (1) American Law Institute, *A Model Code of Pre-Arraignment Procedure: Proposed Official Draft* (Philadelphia: The American Law Institute, 1975) Sec. SS 290.2 (2) which would allow the admission of illegally seized evidence unless the violation of Fourth Amendment rights was "substantial" or otherwise required by federal or state constitutions; (2) U.S. Congress, Senate, *A bill to amend Title 18 of the United States Code to define and limit the exclusionary rule in Federal criminal proceedings,* Ninety-third Congress, First session, 1973, S. 881, a bill introduced by Senator Bentsen which, based on the American Law Institute proposal, would allow the admission in federal criminal proceedings of evidence which had been obtained in violation of the Fourth Amendment, unless the court, having considered all the circumstances surrounding the search, concluded that the violation had been "substantial"; (3) *Bivens* v. *Six Unknown Named Agents of Federal Bureau of Narcotics* 403 U.S. 388, 411-427 (1971) in which Burger, C.J., in his dissent called upon Congress to adopt a tort remedy in lieu of the exclusionary rule.

4. Richard A. Edwards, "Criminal Liability for Unreasonable Searches and Seizures," *Virginia Law Review* 41 (1955):621-632; Caleb Foote, "Tort Remedies for Police Violations of Individual Rights," *Minnesota Law Review* 39 (1955):493-516; "Grievance Response Mechanisms for Police Misconduct," *Virginia Law Review* 55 (1969):909-951; AELE Law Enforcement Legal Defense Center, *Survey of Police Misconduct Litigation 1967-1971* (Evanston, Ill.: Americans for Effective Law Enforcement, 1974); James R. Hudson, "Police Review Boards and Police Accountability," *Law and Contemporary Problems* 36 (1971):515-538.

5. Dallin H. Oaks, "Studying the Exclusionary Rule in Search and Seizure," *University of Chicago Law Review* 37 (1970):665-757; "Search and Seizure in Illinois: Enforcement of the Constitutional Right of Privacy," *Northwestern University Law Review* 47 (1952):493-507; James E. Spiotto, "Search and Seizure: An Empirical Study of the Exclusionary Rule and its Alternatives," *The Journal of Legal Studies* 2 (1973):243-278; "On the Limitations of Empirical Evaluations of the Exclusionary Rule: A Critique of the Spiotto Research and *United States* v. *Calandra*," *Northwestern University Law Review* 69 (1974):740-798; Bradley C. Canon, "Is the Exclusionary Rule in Failing Health? Some New Data and a Plea Against a Precipitous Conclusion," *Kentucky Law Journal* 62 (1974):681-730.

6. *Wolf* v. *Colorado* 338 U.S. 25, 41-47 (1948), Murphy J., dissenting; Jack B. Weinstein, "Local Responsibility for Improvement of Search and Seizure Practices," *Rocky Mountain Law Review* 34 (1962):150-180; Stuart S. Nagel, "Testing the Effects of Excluding Illegally Seized Evidence," *Wisconsin Law Review* (1965):283-310; Michael Katz, "The Supreme Court and the States: An Inquiry into *Mapp* v. *Ohio* in North Carolina; The Model, the Study and the Implications," *North Carolina Law Review* 45 (1966): 119-151; Gary Friedman, "The Impact of *Mapp* v. *Ohio* on Fairfield County," *Connecticut Bar Journal* 40 (1966): 118-132.

7. For the effects on arrest and conviction rates, see, e.g., Canon, "Failing Health?"; Katz, "*Mapp* v. *Ohio* in North Carolina"; Oaks, "Studying the Exclusionary Rule." For the effects on police reports on the reasons for arrest, see, e.g., "Effect of *Mapp* v. *Ohio* on Police Search and Seizure Practices in Narcotics cases," *Columbia Journal of Law and Social Problems* 4 (1968):87-104. For the effects on use of courtroom time, see, e.g., Oaks, "Studying the Exclusionary Rule." For the effects on issuance of search warrants, see, e.g., Canon, "Failing Health?" For use of the participant observation method of research see, e.g., Jerome H. Skolnick, *Justice Without Trial* (New York: John Wiley and Sons, 1967).

8. 414 U.S. 338, 348 n.5 (1974).

9. "We find ourselves, therefore, in no better position than the Court was in 1960, when it said: 'Empirical statistics are not available . . . ' (*Elkins* v. *U.S.*)." *U.S.* v. *Janis* 428 U.S. 433, 453 (1976). "Despite the absence of supportive empirical evidence, we have assumed that the immediate effect of

exclusion will be to discourage law enforcement officials from violating the Fourth Amendment by removing the incentive to disregard it." *Stone, Warden* v. *Powell* 428 U.S. 465, 492 (1976).

10. In other words, those conducted in accordance with, or in violation of, the Fourth Amendment.

11. See, e.g., *Camara* v. *Municipal Court* 387 U.S. 523, 528-529 (1967); *McDonald* v. *U.S.* 335 U.S. 451, 453 (1948); *Johnson* v. *U.S.* 333 U.S. 10, 14 (1948).

2 Literary and Legal Framework

History of the Exclusionary Rule

Of all the means for ensuring compliance with Fourth Amendment rights none is as controversial as the exclusionary rule. Stated simply the rule requires that no evidence seized as the result of an illegal search shall be admissible in court.[1] It is part of a wider framework that requires the exclusion of evidence obtained in violation of other amendments as well.[2]

One of the rule's earliest appearances was in the case of *Boyd* v. *U.S.* in which the Supreme Court faced the question of whether the defendant's failure to produce certain private papers could, in accordance with the terms of a revenue statute, be construed by the trial court as a confession of a charge of fraud. The Court held that the compulsory production of the papers resulting from the provisions of the statute violated the defendant's rights against both self-incrimination and unreasonable search and seizure. In this case the Fourth and Fifth Amendments were stated to "run almost into each other,"[3] and the evidence was held to have been wrongfully admitted.

In 1914, twenty-eight years later, the Supreme Court for the first time excluded evidence solely on the basis of a violation of the defendant's Fourth Amendment rights. In *Weeks* v. *U.S.*[4] the Court held as inadmissible correspondence seized in the defendant's house during his absence and without his authority by a United States marshal who had a warrant neither for his arrest nor for a search of the premises. "To sanction such proceedings," the Court stated, "would be to affirm by Judicial decision a manifest neglect if not an open defiance of the prohibitions of the Constitution. . . ."[5] The Court, it must be noted, was dealing with a federal case and it is not clear from the opinion whether the result was felt to be mandated by the Constitution or the Court's special supervisory powers over federal officials. Whatever the basis for the decision, the Court's ruling did not apply to the states. Indeed, at this date the Fourth Amendment had not yet been held to apply to the states.

In 1949 in *Wolf* v. *Colorado,* the Court moved part way toward such a ruling when it held that "the security of one's privacy against arbitrary intrusion by the police—which is at the core of the Fourth Amendment—is basic to a free society. It is therefore implicit in 'the concept of ordered liberty' and as such enforceable against the states through the Due Process Clause."[6]

Reviewing the *Weeks* decision, the Court found it to be "not derived from the explicit requirements of the Fourth Amendment" but to be "a matter of judicial implication."[7] Since most of the English-speaking world did not regard the exclusion of evidence as an essential ingredient of the right against arbitrary police intrusion, since other remedies existed, and since, as of that date thirty-one states rejected the *Weeks* doctrine while only sixteen were in agreement with it, the Court concluded that it could not "condemn as falling below the minimal standards assured by the Due Process clause a State's reliance upon other methods which if consistently enforced, would be equally effective."[8]

As a result of the decision in *Wolf*, the exclusionary rule remained applicable only to evidence illegally seized by federal officials which was sought for introduction in federal court. Two parallel developments, however, widened the scope of the rule.

In 1952 in *Rochin* v. *California*[9] the Court introduced a narrow version of the exclusionary rule in state criminal proceedings. Evidence that had been obtained in a manner which "shocked the conscience" was held to violate the Due Process clause of the Fourteenth Amendment and no longer to be admissible in state criminal proceedings. In *Irvine* v. *California*,[10] with Justice Frankfurter (the author of the majority opinion in *Rochin*) and three other justices dissenting, the holding in *Rochin* was limited to cases involving coercion, violence or brutality to the person.

In 1956 in *Rea* v. *U.S.*[11] the Court, through use of its supervisory powers over federal law enforcement agencies, enjoined a federal officer from handing over illegally seized evidence to state authorities for use in a state prosecution and from giving testimony concerning the evidence. In 1960 in *Elkins* v. *U.S.*[12] the Court overturned the so-called "silver platter"doctrine, which states that evidence of a federal crime found by state police during an illegal search for a state crime could be turned over to federal authorities as long as federal officials did not take part in the search but merely received the illegal evidence on a "silver platter."

As a result of these decisions, evidence illegally seized by federal officials was inadmissible in federal courts, evidence that had been illegally seized by federal officials could not be used in state courts, and evidence illegally seized by state officials could not be used in federal courts. The only instance in which illegally seized evidence was admissible was when it had been seized by state officials and introduced in state proceedings. Even here it would be inadmissible if it had been seized in a manner that "shocked the conscience" and involved coercion, violence, or brutality to the person.

In 1961 the Supreme Court, arguably stretching the case to fit its decision,[13] closed "the only courtroom door remaining open to evidence secured by official lawlessness"[14] and held in *Mapp* v. *Ohio* that "all evidence obtained by searches and seizures in violation of the Constitution is, by that same authority, inadmissible in a State Court."[15] While *Weeks* was seen to have been "constitutionally required—even if judicially implied,"[16] *Wolf* had been "bottomed on factual considerations" which no longer applied.[17] Significance was placed on the fact that state practice was no longer as opposed to the exclusionary rule as before. Despite *Wolf*, more than half the states passing upon the exclusionary rule since that date had wholly or partly adopted or adhered to the *Weeks* rule. Most important, however, was the Court's finding of the worthlessness of the "other means of protection," on whose existence the majority in *Wolf* had so relied for their decision.[18] "The experience of California that such other remedies have been worthless and futile," the Court stated, "is buttressed by the experience of other states."[19] Without the exclusionary rule the Fourth Amendment's right of privacy would be a "form of words."[20] "To hold otherwise" the Court declared, "is to grant the right but in reality to withhold its privilege and enjoyment."[21]

With the decision in *Mapp*, the exclusionary rule was mandated a Constitutional requirement in state criminal proceedings. Arguably, however, the Fourth Amendment was not made totally applicable to the states until the Court's decision in *Ker* v. *California* two years later.[22]

In recent years the Supreme Court has impinged to some extent upon both the scope and vitality of the exclusionary rule. For example, in 1973 the Court held in *U.S.* v. *Robinson*[23] that an arrest for a traffic violation justifies a full search of the arrestee's person for contraband unrelated to the traffic offense. In 1974 in *Calandra* v. *U.S.*[24] it held that the exclusionary rule was not applicable in grand jury proceedings. In 1976 in *Stone, Warden* v. *Powell*[25] it held that habeas corpus petitions challenging the right of state authorities to hold a prisoner in custody cannot be considered by the federal courts when such petitions are based on asserted Fourth Amendment rights, and the state prisoner has been given the opportunity to fully and fairly litigate his Fourth Amendment claims. Despite this trend, the exclusionary rule still remains in force, and an unreasonable search and seizure will still result in the exclusion of the illegally seized evidence at trial.

Alternatives to the Exclusionary Rule: Their Drawbacks

The history of the exclusionary rule thus shows that the Court adopted it as the primary means of sanctioning police behavior because of the failure of other legal procedures to safeguard Fourth Amendment rights. These other legal procedures consist of criminal and civil actions against errant police officials. If successful, these sanctions would punish the errant police official by imposing a criminal penalty or an order to pay compensation, and discourage other police officials from indulging in similar actions. The tort action would, additionally, it should be noted, provide the victim of an illegal search with monetary compensation.

In addition to these legal sanctions there are administrative procedures which would also, if successful, control and discipline police officials and deter them from making illegal searches and seizures. Each of these devices is examined to discover why they have been considered ineffective in protecting Fourth Amendment rights.

Criminal sanctions include both state and federal actions against police officers. While these procedures allow for the errant official to be punished and for the illegally seized evidence to be presented at the trial of the victim of the unreasonable search and seizure, they possess features that cause them to be infrequently used.

In a criminal case the police are responsible for the initial investigation into the alleged criminal conduct. In cases where the alleged wrongdoer is a police officer, however, the investigating officer may find it difficult to carry out a totally impartial investigation. Prosecutors, moreover, have been unwilling to take action against errant officers because of their reluctance to antagonize an agency with which they must work closely. Even when a case has been brought to trial it is often found that the jury is unwilling to convict. Natural sympathy with the police officer, who is seen as "merely trying to do his job," may result in a finding of reasonable doubt as to the officer's guilt. This is likely when malice or intent must be proved.

In his 1955 survey of the use of criminal provisions, Edwards found that a federal statute establishing criminal liability on the part of one who improperly procured a search warrant had existed for forty years without being the source of a single conviction. Furthermore there was no reported case, under a 1921 amendment to the National Prohibition Law, which established criminal liability for officers making illegal searches, despite the fact that search and seizure litigation had then reached an unprecedented peak.[26] In a survey published that year, Caleb Foote found only a handful of state criminal false imprisonment prosecutions of police officers in the preceding fifteen years and not one criminal trespass prosecution as a result of an illegal search and seizure.[27]

Civil sanctions include state tort actions against both state and federal officials, a federal cause of action against state officials under 42 U.S.C. Section 1983, a Constitutional tort action against federal officials under the Supreme Court's holding in *Bivens* v. *Six Unknown Named Agents of Federal Bureau of Narcotics*,[28] and an action against the federal government under an amendment to the Federal Tort Claims Act.[29]

State tort actions, such as those for trespass, false imprisonment, or assault are, in their present form, generally agreed to be highly ineffective.[30] Numerous reasons are advanced in support of this conclusion. Cost may prevent some potential plaintiffs from bringing suit. Others may be deterred by fear of police reprisals. Still others may be barred by "civil death." When suit is brought, the plaintiff faces many legal obstacles. To begin with the police official is allowed a broad defense of privilege by state rules. Moreover, since a law official stands in essence as a private citizen in such an action, some acts, though unconstitutional, may not be actionable. As the Court stated in *Bivens*, "The interests protected by state laws regulating trespass and the invasion of privacy, and those protected by the Fourth Amendment's guarantee against unreasonable searches and seizures, may be inconsistent or even hostile."[31] Thus, under state law a federal official, like a private citizen, is not generally liable in trespass if he demands and is granted entry to another's house.

As in the criminal action, juries are likely to sympathize with the police officer rather than a claimant who is regarded as undeserving. "Juries in such cases are not apt to be very sympathetic to the run-of-the-mill dope peddler, petty thief, or gambler against whom the overwhelming number of police infractions are committed."[32] Even when the plaintiff obtains a successful judgment, there are impediments to his receiving much in the way of compensation. While damages in a trespass action are generally limited to the extent of injury to physical property, and do not cover pain and suffering, state rules allowing the liberal admission of evidence in mitigation of damages may severely reduce the amount recovered in other cases. Punitive damages, if awarded, may be difficult to obtain since it would be necessary to prove malice on the part of the police officer, who would be presumed to be acting out of a sense of duty.[33] Finally, since actual recovery of damages depends on finding non-exempt assets to satisfy the judgment, and since police officers are not notoriously wealthy defendants, a successful plaintiff may find that he has received an empty judgment.

In view of all the obstacles in the way of a plaintiff in a state tort action, it is not surprising that it is an infrequently used remedy. Foote noted that the action for false imprisonment appeared to have greater effect than the action for trespass because of the inflation of the measure of damages often allowed in the former. Finding only one reported trespass case in the previous ten years, he concluded that the trespass remedy was completely impotent.[34] A 1952 study found in its compilation of tort actions in appellate courts only forty cases between 1814 and 1949.[35]

According to 42 U.S.C. Section 1983:

> Every person who, under color of any statute, ordinance, regulation, custom, or usage, of any State or Territory, subjects or causes to be subjected, any citizen of the United States or other person within the jurisdiction thereof to the deprivation of any rights, privileges, or immunities secured by the Constitution and laws, shall be liable to the party injured in an action at law, suit in equity, or other proper proceeding for redress.[36]

Section 1983 applies only to state officials. The possibility of an action against a municipality was limited by the decision in *Monroe* v. *Pape*[37] which held that a municipal corporation was not a person under the statute and therefore could not be sued. In this form the Section 1983 remedy has proved little more effective than the state tort action."Jury reluctance and the insufficient measure of damages are probably the outstanding difficulties."[38] Injunctions have occasionally been issued under the section. It is rare, however, that such a remedy is appropriate. Few search victims receive advance notice of the search and an injunction can provide little help once the search has occurred. Statistical evidence showing the infrequency of the Section 1983 actions in this area is adduced by the finding that only fifty-three actions were entertained between the years 1951 and 1968.[39]

The Supreme Court's decision in *Bivens*[40] provided aggrieved individuals with a federal action against federal officials which was similar in nature to the federal cause of action for damages available against state officials under 42 U.S.C. Section 1983. Though arming a potential plaintiff with an additional weapon, the decision may have little practical effect, for there is little in the remedy to suggest that it differs much from the other civil remedies discussed previously.[41]

Though there is evidence that the number of suits initiated against police officers and law enforcement agencies is increasing, the success rate of these suits remains small. A survey conducted by the International Association of Chiefs of Police, which examined both state and federal civil suits brought against the police during the years 1967-1971, found that in only 3.8% of the cases was the plaintiff successful. In over 80% of the cases the suit was filed in state court.[42]

In 1974 an amendment to the Federal Tort Claims Act was passed which waived sovereign immunity and allowed an action against the federal government for the infringement of Fourth Amendment rights by federal law enforcement officials.[43] Though it overcomes some of the obstacles to a viable tort remedy (for example, by not providing for jury trial), it is somewhat limited and still contains certain familiar procedural defects. Thus, the claim must be for damage, loss of property, death, or personal injury; the damage must have been the result of a negligent or wrongful act; such act must have been committed by a federal employee; the employee must have been acting within the scope of employment; and the circumstances must be such that a private person would be liable under state law if such a person committed the act. There is, moreover, no provision for payment of attorney fees.[44]

Available administrative procedures consist primarily of internal police review and external review by civilian review boards. Although internal police review boards are a common feature in police departments throughout the country, they are generally distrusted by the public. It is felt that if a citizen files a complaint, a fair outcome is unlikely because he or she is dependent upon the police both to investigate and to make a decision upon that complaint. The police will naturally back up their fellow officers, especially if they are perceived to have merely been carrying out police duties.

The Crime Commission's Task Force Report on the Police reported that frequently an "officer's behavior is clearly illegal or improper, but is consistent with the routine practice of the particular agency and is generally condoned by the administration."[45] In his discussion of the New York City Police Review Board, Chevigny noted that the inquiry was not focused on the existence of probable cause for the police action taken, but rather on the existence of "good faith": if the police officers "were doing their job by police standards, that is, if they were really trying to investigate crime, they would be given the widest latitude. The mere fact that they violated constitutional rights in the process of enforcing the laws was not a ground for discipline."[46] In the case of the Chicago Police Department, ". . . if a search and seizure incident is neither egregious nor brutal, a citizen's complaint would probably not result in disciplinary action."[47] Even when disciplinary action is taken, it is likely to be token punishment that will tend to exasperate rather than satisfy the grievant.[48]

Experience with civilian review boards has generally been stormy,[49] but there is evidence that they may be more trusted by the public than the internal police review boards. For example, the New York Civilian Complaint Review Board "received 440 complaints during its four-month existence, compared to the approximate annual average of 200 received by the police-operated complaint review board prior to 1966."[50] However, the boards have merely possessed advisory powers and for the most part have relied on the police for investigative work. They have, moreover, incurred the opposition of police organizations, which have resented outside interference in police affairs. In New York City the opposition of the Police Benevolent Association, and in Philadelphia the opposition of the Fraternal Order of Police, were primarily responsible for the demise of the civilian board.

Procedural defects and other impediments have thus rendered both criminal and civil actions ineffective in controlling and disciplining police officials. Their infrequent use draws into question their potential as deterrents. Civil actions have also been unsuccessful in providing the victims of illegal searches and seizures with compensation. While internal police review procedures have suffered from public distrust, civilian review boards have been the victims of police opposition.

These procedures have all been subjected to negative comment and criticism. The exclusionary rule, in which so much trust was placed as a last resort, has itself not been free from attack. Indeed, the rule may be the most costly of all in terms of detriment to the process of law enforcement; for while other procedures are merely ineffective in accomplishing their objectives, the exclusionary rule brings in addition many negative side effects.

Negative Effects of the Exclusionary Rule

Two theoretical justifications lie behind the exclusionary rule. The first, which may be called the judicial integrity or normative rationale, states that the courts should not participate in illegal behavior by using evidence obtained by it.[51] The second, which may be called the deterrent or factual rationale, presents the theory that if the courts exclude evidence that has been illegally seized, police officials will be deterred from violating the Fourth Amendment's prohibition against unreasonable searches and seizures.[52] While focusing in earlier cases on the judicial integrity rationale,[53] the Supreme Court may be seen, since its decision in *Mapp*,[54] to be advancing the deterrent rationale as the main, if not the sole, theoretical justification for the exclusionary rule.[55]

Like the previously discussed procedures, the exclusionary rule has been stated to possess many drawbacks. Foremost among these is the fact that it sets free the guilty, but does not compensate the innocent. "It protects one against whom incriminating evidence is discovered, but does nothing to protect innocent persons who are the victims of illegal, but fruitless searches."[56] Suppression of physical evidence which "is no less reliable when illegally obtained,"[57] suggests the wholesale release of certain types of defendants. Studies of Chicago courts indicate that in 1950 the motion to suppress was dispositive for 76% of defendants charged with gambling offenses, 19% of those charged with narcotics offenses, and 25% of those charged with carrying concealed weapons;[58] while in 1969 the figures were 45%, 33%, and 24%,[59] and 24%, 36%, and 22% in 1971.[60]

It is also alleged that the exclusionary rule neither punishes nor affects the errant police official. "The immediate sanction triggered by the application of the rule is visited upon the prosecutor whose case against a criminal is either weakened or destroyed entirely. The doctrine deprives the police in no real sense."[61] The mistake has been in regarding the law enforcement process as a monolithic enterprise. The fact is that "the police are often not so much concerned with convictions as with arrests and case clearances."[62]

Even when a police official desires to ensure that evidence will not be excluded because he has made an illegal search, the complexity of the laws of search and seizure may prevent him from understanding the scope of his legal authority. When a significant decision is rendered on the topic of search and seizure, the police are often not informed of the decision or its possible effect on their behavior. When a police officer appears in court and the motion to suppress is either granted or denied, he will in most cases receive no elaboration of the ruling. When he hears the court decision, he "usually departs with a bewildered expression on his face; seldom does he have any clearer understanding of the limitations on his authority than he had prior to the hearing."[63] In addition, he may well be bemused by the varying definitions of "reasonableness" and by the fact that "what is 'reasonable' to a judge in a narcotics case is not 'reasonable' to the *same* judge in a gambling case."[64]

A further drawback to the exclusionary rule is that it is inflexible. In the words of Chief Justice Burger, it inflicts "universal 'capital punishment' "[65] upon all evidence illegally seized. It is sensitive neither to the seriousness of the violation nor to the police motive involved, be it harmless or malicious.

The rule, requiring special suppression hearings, causes delay and diverts attention from the question of the guilt or innocence of the defendant. Indeed, with the court focusing on his behavior, the police officer may begin to think that he is the one on trial. A study in January 1970 on the use of court time, revealed that motions to suppress accounted for 20% of the courtroom time in the rackets branch and 34% of the time in the narcotics branch of the Chicago Circuit Court.[66] Further drawbacks to the exclusionary rule lie in the undesirable effects it may have on plea bargaining[67] and on the undesirable changes it may cause in the substantive law, such as broadening the legal definition of "reasonable"[68] or "probable cause."[69]

Much is heard about how the rule "handcuffs the police." It has been stated that this whole argument should be abandoned and that "if this is a negative effect, then it is an effect of the constitutional rules, not an effect of the exclusionary rule as the means chosen for their enforcement."[70] Whatever the merits of this stance, it does seem that subjective police attitudes about the exclusionary rule have led some officers to engage in questionable practices in order to bypass the rule's effects.

Some police officials, it is believed, "bend" the facts in order to avoid the suppression of evidence and help obtain convictions. Faced with the likelihood that the court will rule that evidence seized has been illegally obtained and thus will be inadmissible at trial, a police officer may decide to perjure himself rather than see a guilty defendant let go because of lack of admissible evidence. A study of misdemeanor narcotic offenses in New York City over four periods, one preceding and three following the *Mapp* decision, examined police officer allegations regarding the discovery of evidence. It showed, without any other apparent explanation, a decrease in the percentage of hidden contraband and an increase in the percentage of contraband dropped or in plain view. The study concluded that suspicious changes in arrest data after the *Mapp* decision clearly indicated that many police allegations had been altered in order to fit the *Mapp* requirements.[71]

A second questionable practice that may be fostered by the exclusionary rule is police imposition of extrajudicial punishment. The concern is that the police may be so hampered by the exclusionary rule that they cannot obtain the convictions they require and as a result "they will be tempted to harrass suspects, to inflict extra-legal punishment."[72] Thus unable to obtain successful convictions, the police may, for instance, simply try to make life difficult for narcotics addicts.

A final drawback to the exclusionary rule is the allegation that it may allow the police "to immunize a criminal from prosecution by deliberately overstepping legal bounds in obtaining vital evidence."[73] Observation of courtroom events leading to the release of a high proportion of defendants in gambling cases in Chicago in 1950 led one writer to conclude that the raids were made to immunize the gamblers, and at the same time satisfy the public that the gamblers were subject to police harrassment.[74]

Choosing Among Negatives

The discussion has centered thus far on the negative aspects of the procedures examined. The picture evokes images of criminal and civil actions, rarely employed, of administrative procedures that rubberstamp police behavior or are rendered impotent by police opposition, and of an exclusionary rule adopted as a last resort and full of imperfections.

Before evaluating the contribution that could be made by these procedures, a decision must be made as to what can logically be expected from each of them. Two major considerations were listed in the introduction: first, protecting the general public by deterring governmental officials from conducting illegal searches; and second, when such protection has been insufficient, punishment of the errant officials and compensation of the wronged individuals.

State or federal tort actions seem to be the most suitable for compensating individuals who have been illegally searched. They alone, for the most part, can provide monetary as well as psychological satisfaction.[75] Various modifications have been suggested which would render them more potent. Successful claimants could be paid reasonable attorneys' fees.[76] The government and municipalities could be made liable for the wrongful actions of their officials.[77] Such officials could be insured.[78] Minimum fixed damages could be set.[79] Special jury instructions could be created or jury use abolished.[80] An alternative proposition would establish administrative bodies to hear and deal with claims presented by the victims of illegal searches.[81]

If regularly invoked, tort actions could also fulfill the function of punishing or disciplining errant officials. However, the method of assessing tort damages makes such usage of the procedure inappropriate. Since the amount of damages is determined by the harm occasioned and not by the culpability of the wrongdoer, a minor infringement of an individual's rights could prove very costly for the offending officer while a major infringement might not. In this respect, criminal proceedings might be more appropriate. A special prosecutor with an independent investigative force might obviate many of the difficulties in the traditional criminal procedure.[82] Criminal prosecution is, however, a serious proceeding, implying society's moral judgment and, in the case of conviction, condemnation. Because many violations of Fourth Amendment rights may be either insubstantial or inadvertent, the invocation of such a sanction seems unlikely and unjustified except in the most serious cases.

The use of internal police procedures to discipline errant police officials has been criticized on the grounds that illegal behavior may be condoned rather than punished, since police norms may be out of tune with and unsympathetic to legal requirements. To counteract outside distrust of internal review, it has been suggested that complaints should be actively encouraged, rather than discouraged; that all complaints should be accepted initially, and investigative work be done by special internal investigative units; that hearings be open to the public; that quasi-judicial procedures be followed and that decisions be fully publicized.[83] As with criminal prosecution, however, the only compensation received by an illegally searched person would be psychological.

The extent to which the police view the exclusion of illegally seized evidence as a matter of personal discipline appears to be minimal, but until now we could only speculate on these views. Oaks points out that while the exclusionary rule does not fulfill a specific deterrent function (since it does not directly punish the errant officer), the officer's future actions may be affected by his disappointment at seeing an offender let go because of a lack of admissible evidence.[84]

The whole topic of deterrence, either specific or general, is difficult at best, involving questions of human motivation and compliance, and both short and long-range effects. In all probability the present infrequent invocation of civil and criminal actions renders them highly ineffective as deterrent mechanisms, while the indirect effect of the exclusionary rule makes its potential questionable. If internal police review in most cases simply condones illegal police behavior, then it does not even attempt to act as a deterrent. As yet, no detailed research has attempted to gauge how police, defense, or prosecution officials view these procedures.

Notes

1. This is subject to such exceptions as when an accused lacks standing to invoke the exclusionary rule (*Jones* v. *U.S.* 362 U.S. 257 [1960]) or when the evidence is used to impeach the testimony of a defendant who takes the stand on his own behalf (*Walder* v. *United States* 347 U.S. 62 [1954]). In addition the exclusionary rule does not apply to grand jury proceedings (*U.S.* v. *Calandra* 414 U.S. 338 [1974]).

2. For example, *Miranda* v. *Arizona* 384 U.S. 436 (1966) (Fifth Amendment privilege against self incrimination); *Escobedo* v. *Illinois* 378 U.S. 478 (1964); *U.S.* v. *Wade* 338 U.S. 218 (1967) (Sixth Amendment right to counsel); *Rochin* v. *California* 342 U.S. 165 (1952) (Fourteenth Amendment right to due process).

3. 116 U.S. 616, 630 (1886).

4. 232 U.S. 383 (1914).

5. Ibid. at 394.

6. 338 U.S. 25, 27-28 (1949).

7. Ibid. at 28.

8. Ibid.

9. 342 U.S. 165 (1952).

10. 347 U.S. 128 (1954).

11. 350 U.S. 214 (1956).

12. 364 U.S. 206 (1960).

13. As stated by Mr. Justice Harlan in his dissent with which Justices Frankfurter and Whittaker joined: "... the new and pivotal issue brought to the Court by this appeal is whether ... making criminal the *mere* knowing possession or control of obscene material ... is consistent with the rights of free thought and expression assured against state action by the Fourteenth Amendment. That was the principal issue which was decided by the Ohio Supreme Court, which was tendered by appellant's jurisdictional statement, and which was briefed and argued in this Court. In this posture of things, I think it fair to say that five members of this Court have simply 'reached out' to overrule *Wolf.*" *Mapp* v. *Ohio* 367 U.S. 643, 673-677 (1961).

14. *Mapp* v. *Ohio* 367 U.S. 643, 654-655 (1961).

15. Ibid. at 655.

16. Ibid. at 648.

17. Ibid. at 651.

18. Ibid.

19. Ibid. at 652.

20. Ibid at 655.

21. Ibid. at 656.

22. 374 U.S. 23 (1963). This proposition is supported both by the differential approach taken by the Court in applying its decision to the federal government and to the states and to its references to the right of privacy. "We find that, as to the federal government, the Fourth and Fifth Amendments and, as to the states, the freedom from unconscionable invasions of privacy and the freedom from convictions based upon coerced confessions do enjoy an 'intimate relation' in their perpetuation of 'principles of humanity and civil liberty. . . . ' " *Mapp* v. *Ohio* 367 U.S. 643, 656-657 (1961); "Since the Fourth Amendment's right of privacy has been declared enforceable against the states through the due process clause of the Fourteenth, it is enforceable against them by the same sanction of exclusion as is used against the federal government." Ibid. at 655.

23. 414 U.S. 218 (1973).

24. 414 U.S. 338 (1974).

25. 428 U.S. 465 (1976).

26. Richard A. Edwards, "Criminal Liability for Unreasonable Searches and Seizures," *Virginia Law Review* 41 (1955):626-629.

27. Caleb Foote, "Tort Remedies for Police Violations of Individual Rights," *Minnesota Law Review* 39 (1955):494.

28. 403 U.S. 388 (1971).

29. *United States Code,* Title 28, Section 2680(h) (as amended Mar. 16, 1974, Pub. L. 93-253, Section 2, 88 Stat. 50).

30. See, e.g., Peter Fine, "Private Assumption of the Police Function Under the Fourth Amendment," *Boston University Law Review* 51 (1971):464-482; Foote, "Tort Remedies"; "Grievance Response Mechanisms for Police Misconduct," *Virginia Law Review* 55 (1969):909-951; Michael Gunter, "The Exclusionary Rule in Context," *North Carolina Law Review* 50

(1972): 1049-1079; Carter LaPrade, "An Alternative to the Exclusionary Rule Presently Administered Under the Fourth Amendment," *Connecticut Bar Journal* 48 (1974):100-110; Charles M. Sevilla, "The Exclusionary Rule and Police Perjury," *San Diego Law Review* 11 (1974):839-879; Harvey Wingo, "Growing Disillusionment with the Exclusionary Rule," *Southwestern Law Journal* 25 (1971):573-593.

31. 403 U.S. 388, 394 (1971).

32. Monrad G. Paulsen, "The Exclusionary Rule and Misconduct by the Police," *Journal of Criminal Law, Criminology and Police Science* 52 (1961):260.

33. "Constitutional Law—Federal Agents Conducting Unreasonable Searches and Seizures are Liable for Damages under the Fourth Amendment," *Texas Law Review* 50 (1972):798-800.

34. Foote, "Tort Remedies," p. 498.

35. "Search and Seizure in Illinois: Enforcement of the Constitutional Right of Privacy," *Northwestern University Law Review* 47 (1952):502.

36. *United States Code,* Title 42, Section 1983.

37. 365 U.S. 167 (1961).

38. Dallin H. Oaks, "Studying the Exclusionary Rule in Search and Seizure,"*University of Chicago Law Review* 37 (1970):674. See also "Grievance Response Mechanisms for Police Misconduct," *Virginia Law Review* 55 (1969):925; Emil P. Moschella, "Probable Cause: The Officer's Shield to Suits under the Federal Civil Rights Act," FBI Law Enforcement Bulletin 45 (1976):28.

39. "Constitutional Law—Damages: Unreasonable Search by Federal Agents under Color of Authority Provides a Federal Cause of Action for Damages under the Fourth Amendment," *Brooklyn Law Review* 38 (1971):529.

40. 403 U.S. 388 (1971).

41. The remedy does not avoid the familiar problems of obstacles to bringing an action, of courtroom difficulties, or of barriers to receiving a satisfied judgment. This was in fact recognized by Harlan, J., in his concurring opinion in *Bivens* v. *Six Unknown Named Agents of Federal Bureau of Narcotics* 403 U.S. 388 (1971) when he stated at 411 that: "of course, for a variety of reasons, the remedy may not often be sought." For a more thorough discussion of the potential of the remedy, see, e.g., Richard J. Sabat, "The Fourth Amendment: Is a Lawsuit the Answer?" *Syracuse Law Review* 23 (1972):1244-1246; Michael Billy, Jr. and Gordon A. Rehnborg, Jr., "The Fourth Amendment Exclusionary Rule: Past, Present, No Future," *The American Criminal Law Review* 12 (1975):529-532.

42. AELE Law Enforcement Legal Defense Center, *Survey of Police Misconduct Litigation 1967-71* (Evanston, Ill.: Americans for Effective Law Enforcement, 1974) p. 6.

43. *United States Code,* Title 28, Section 2680(h) (as amended Mar. 16, 1974, Pub. L. 93-253, Section 2, 88 Stat. 50).

44. For a fuller discussion of the 1974 Amendment to the Federal Tort

Claims Act see, e.g., Francis A. Gilligan, "The Federal Tort Claims Act—An Alternative to the Exclusionary Rule?" *The Journal of Criminal Law and Criminology* 66 (1975):1-22.

45. President's Commission on Law Enforcement and Administration of Justice, *Task Force Report: The Police* (Washington, D.C.: U.S. Government Printing Office, 1967) p. 28.

46. Paul G. Chevigny, "Police Abuses in Connection with the Law of Search and Seizure," *Criminal Law Bulletin* 5 (1969):29.

47. James E. Spiotto, "Search and Seizure: An Empirical Study of the Exclusionary Rule and its Alternatives," *The Journal of Legal Studies* 2 (1973):273. For an earlier account of the operation of the internal review and investigation procedures of the Chicago Police Department, see James R. Hudson, "Police Review Boards and Police Accountability," *Law and Contemporary Problems* 36 (1971):519.

48. "Grievance Response Mechanisms," p. 938.

49. For a general account of the history of the Civilian Review Boards, see President's Commission on Law Enforcement and Administration of Justice, *The Police,* (1967) pp. 200-202. For an account of the history of the New York and Philadelphia boards see Hudson, "Police Review Boards," pp. 522-527.

50. "Grievance Response Mechanisms," p. 941.

51. The best expression of this concept is perhaps found in the oft-quoted dissenting opinion of Brandeis, J., in *Olmstead* v. *U.S.* 277 U.S. 438, 485 (1927): "If the government becomes a lawbreaker, it breeds contempt for law; it invites every man to become a law unto himself; it invites anarchy. To declare that in the administration of the Criminal Law the end justifies the means—to declare that the Government may commit crimes in order to secure the conviction of a private criminal—would bring terrible retribution. Against that pernicious doctrine this court should resolutely set its face."

52. A third, but not well supported justification lies in the interrelationship of the Fourth and Fifth Amendments. See *Boyd* v. *U.S.* 116 U.S. 616 (1886); *Mapp* v. *Ohio* 367 U.S. 643, 661-662 (1961) (Black, J., concurring).

53. "To sanction such proceedings would be to affirm by judicial decision a manifest neglect if not an open defiance of the prohibitions of the Constitution, intended for the protection of the people against such unauthorized action." *Weeks* v. *U.S.* 232 U.S. 383, 394 (1914).

54. 367 U.S. 643. In *Mapp* v. *Ohio* 367 U.S. 643, 656 (1961) the court may appear to be reiterating an ambivalence between the two rationales that had been expressed earlier in *Elkins* v. *U.S.* 364 U.S. 206 (1960): "Only last year the Court itself recognized that the purpose of the exclusionary rule 'is to deter—to compel respect for the Constitutional guaranty in the only effectively available way—by removing the incentive to disregard it.' *Elkins* v. *U.S.* at 217"; "But as was said in *Elkins,* there is another consideration—the imperative of judicial integrity. 364 U.S. at 222." *Mapp* at 659.

55. "In rejecting the *Wolf* doctrine as to the exclusionary rule the purpose was to deter the lawless actions of the police and to effectively enforce the Fourth Amendment. That purpose will not at this late date be served by the wholesale release of the guilty victims." *Linkletter* v. *Walker* 381 U.S. 618, 637 (1964); "Instead, the rule's prime purpose is to deter future unlawful police conduct and thereby effectuate the guarantee of the Fourth Amendment against unreasonable search and seizures." *U.S.* v. *Calandra* 414 U.S. 338, 347 (1974); "The primary justification for the exclusionary rule then is the deterrence of police conduct that violates Fourth Amendment rights." *Stone, Warden* v. *Powell* 428 U.S. 465, 486 (1976); "The Court, however, has established that the 'prime purpose' of the rule, if not the sole one, 'is to deter future unlawful police conduct.' " *U.S.* v. *Janis* 428 U.S. 433, 446 (1976).

56. *Irvine* v. *California* 347 U.S. 128, 136.

57. Oaks, "Studying the Exclusionary Rule," p. 737.

58. "Search and Seizure in Illinois," p. 498.

59. Oaks, "Studying the Exclusionary Rule," p. 685.

60. Spiotto, "Search and Seizure," p. 247.

61. *Bivens* v. *Six Unknown Named Agents of Federal Bureau of Narcotics* 403 U.S. 388, 416 (1971).

62. Wingo, "Growing Disillusionment," p. 576. See also Wayne R. LaFave, "Improving Police Performance Through the Exclusionary Rule—Part I: Current Police and Local Court Practices," *Missouri Law Review* 30 (1965):431.

63. LaFave, "Improving Police Performance—Part I," p. 403.

64. *1962 American Bar Association Proceedings on Criminal Law* (1963). Remarks by Kings County, N.Y. District Attorney.

65. *Bivens* v. *Six Unknown Named Agents of Federal Bureau of Narcotics* 403 U.S. 388, 419 (1971).

66. Oaks, "Studying the Exclusionary Rule," p. 744. An analysis by Boker and Corrigan of all hearings on the suppression of evidence conducted under section 1538.5 of the California Penal Code in the Alameda County Superior Court from January 1974 to November 1975 revealed that the average time between arrest and disposition of a suppression motion was 131.21 days. Alys Rae Boker and Carol A. Corrigan, "Making the Constable Culpable: A Proposal to Improve the Exclusionary Rule," *Hastings Law Journal* 27 (1976):1294.

67. Oaks, "Studying the Exclusionary Rule," p. 748; "Excluding the Exclusionary Rule: Congressional Assault on *Mapp* v. *Ohio*," *Georgetown Law Journal* 61 (1973):1458.

68. Oaks, "Studying the Exclusionary Rule," p. 747; Michael Katz, "The Supreme Court and the States: An Inquiry into *Mapp* v. *Ohio* in North Carolina. The Model, the Study and the Implications," *North Carolina Law Review* 45 (1966):131; "Privacy Interest of the Fourth Amendment—Does *Mapp* v. *Ohio* Protect It or Pillage It?," *West Virginia Law Review* 74 (1971-1972):154.

69. "Excluding the Exclusionary Rule," p. 1457.

70. Oaks, "Studying the Exclusionary Rule," p. 754.

71. "Effect of *Mapp* v. *Ohio* on Police Search and Seizure Practices in Narcotics Cases," *Columbia Journal of Law and Social Problems* 4 (1968):87-104.

72. Paulsen, "The Exclusionary Rule and Misconduct," p. 257.

73. Oaks, "Studying the Exclusionary Rule," p. 749.

74. Samuel Dash, "Cracks in the Foundation of Criminal Justice," *Illinois Law Review* 46 (1951):391-392.

75. This is not to suggest that provisions allowing for monetary compensation could not be attached either to criminal or disciplinary proceedings. The award of monetary compensation would, however, be a secondary rather than primary objective of the proceeding.

76. Edward J. Horowitz, "Excluding the Exclusionary Rule—Can There be an Effective Alternative?" *Los Angeles Bar Bulletin* 47 (1972):122; William J. Cox, "The Decline of the Exclusionary Rule: An Alternative to Injustice," *Southwestern University Law Review* 4 (1972):80; "Grievance Response Mechanisms," p. 927.

77. Horowitz, "Excluding the Exclusionary Rule," p. 95; Cox, "Decline of the Exclusionary Rule," p.81; "Grievance Response Mechanisms," pp. 909-926; "Search and Seizure in Illinois," p. 504; Foote, "Tort Remedies," p. 514; Kingsley A. Taft, "Protecting the Public from *Mapp* v. *Ohio* without Amending the Constitution," *American Bar Association Journal* 50 (1964):817; Frank J. McGarr, "The Exclusionary Rule: An Ill-Conceived and Ineffective Remedy," *Journal of Criminal Law, Criminology and Police Science* 52 (1961):268; "Federal Agents Liable for Damages," p. 802; Walter E. Dellinger, "Of Rights and Remedies: The Constitution as a Sword," *Harvard Law Review* 85 (1972):1558; Harvey Robert Levin, "An Alternative to the Exclusionary Rule for Fourth Amendment Violations." *Judicature* 58 (1974):76; "Constitutional Law—Search and Seizure—Federal Cause of Action for an Illegal Search and Seizure," *Duquesne Law Review* 10 (1972):710; LaPrade, "An Alternative to the Exclusionary Rule," p. 107.

78. Horowitz, "Excluding the Exclusionary Rule," p. 122; Levin, "An Alternative to the Exclusionary Rule," p. 76.

79. Cox, "Decline of the Exclusionary Rule," p. 80; Foote, "Tort Remedies," p. 501; Horowitz, "Excluding the Exclusionary Rule," p. 122; Levin, "An Alternative to the Exclusionary Rule," p. 76; "Grievance Response Mechanisms," p. 926; "Tort Alternative to the Exclusionary Rule in Search and Seizure," *Journal of Criminal Law, Criminology and Police Science* 63 (1972):263; Sabat, "Is a Lawsuit the Answer," p. 1246.

80. Horowitz, "Excluding the Exclusionary Rule," p. 94; Oaks, "Studying the Exclusionary Rule," p. 718; "Constitutional Law—Searches and Seizures—Fourth Amendment Does Not Establish FederalCause of Action for Damages Caused by an Unreasonable Search and Seizure," *Harvard Law Review* 83 (1970):689; "Federal Agents Liable for Damages," p. 805.

81. Horowitz, "Excluding the Exclusionary Rule," p. 122; Burger, C.J., in his dissent in *Bivens* v. *Six Unknown Named Agents of Federal Bureau of Narcotics*, 403 U.S. 388, 411-427 (1971); for a criticism of Burger's proposal see: Gunter, "Exclusionary Rule in Context," p. 1069.

82. "Search and Seizure in Illinois," p. 505.

83. "Grievance Response Mechanisms," pp. 936-937.

84. Oaks, "Studying the Exclusionary Rule," pp. 709-710.

3 Theoretical Framework

Before investigating the opinions and insights of various criminal justice officials as to means of protecting Fourth Amendment rights, a theoretical framework must be developed to which these opinions and insights can be related. A useful starting point is a typology of searches.

Four types of searches involving Fourth Amendment considerations may be envisaged. As depicted in Figure 3-1 they are: (a) searches conducted in accordance with the Fourth Amendment which reveal contraband or incriminating evidence; (b) searches conducted in accordance with the Fourth Amendment which reveal neither contraband nor incriminating evidence; (c) searches conducted in violation of the Fourth Amendment which reveal contraband or incriminating evidence; and (d) searches conducted in violation of the Fourth Amendment which reveal neither contraband nor incriminating evidence.

The line dividing the population of searches into reasonable and unreasonable, (that is, those conducted in accordance with the Fourth Amendment and those conducted in violation of the Fourth Amendment), is the product of court decisions which have amplified the meaning of the Fourth Amendment. On a case-by-case basis these decisions have sought to strike a balance between the competing interests of law enforcement and civil liberty.

One objective of this study is to locate the position of this line as mandated by the courts in selected cases and to discover the reactions of police officials and defense and prosecution lawyers to its location. Thus envisaging a tension between the interests of law enforcement and those of civil liberty, with the law enforcement interests seeking a wider definition of reasonableness, and civil liberty interests a narrower one, an attempt is made to locate the place where each of the groups draws the boundary between reasonable and unreasonable searches. Using six cases, a summed personal assessment (reasonable) score is obtained for each individual, and differences both within and between groups are examined. It was hypothesized that, in accordance with the demands of their respective roles, police would find more searches reasonable than prosecutors, and prosecutors more than defense lawyers. Of special significance is the relationship between each group mean score and the judicial decision, which indicates which group profile the courts most resemble in their decisions. It will also enable the courts to see how others view their decisions, and guide them by indicating what others consider reasonable or unreasonable searches.

By examining subjective assessments of how cases should be decided, and comparing these assessments with projections of how courts would decide the cases and how they actually did decide them, measures of respondents' perceived

25

Search Legally Reasonable

		Yes	No
Yes		a	c
No		b	d

Evidence Found[a]

[a]This refers to whether any incriminating evidence or contraband is found, irrespective of whether the incriminating evidence or contraband is a sine qua non for conviction of the suspect. This aspect of the necessity of the evidence for conviction will be examined in chapter six.

Figure 3-1. Theoretical Framework

and actual agreement with court decisions are obtained. By asking police officers what they would do, and defense and prosecution officials what they believe police officers would do in the cases presented, a feeling for the "on-street" situation is acquired.

Unlike the marking of the boundary between reasonableness and unreasonableness, which must reflect a value judgment, the division of searches into those which result in the discovery of contraband or incriminating evidence and those which do not is a matter of hard fact. No data on this division, however, is available.

A second objective of this study is to see how respondents estimate the percentage of searches that fail to uncover either contraband or incriminating evidence. Though the police might be expected to give the most accurate picture of the situation, it is instructive to compare their estimates with those of defense and prosecution officials. By asking each group to estimate the percentage of unproductive police searches, we learn how each group views the situation. Because of their different law enforcement interests, it is possible that defense attorneys would estimate a larger number of unproductive searches than would prosecution officials. The police themselves might be expected to give the lowest estimate, but this finding could be affected by the ability of the police to make a more realistic appraisal of the situation. Whether or not each group's estimates of the actual situation are realistic, they indicate how large the issue of unproductive police searches is seen to be.

By combining each group's estimates of the percentage of unproductive police searches with their summed personal assessment score, we may obtain profiles of each group's views on warrantless search and seizure. These profiles may well help place views on the exclusionary rule and discipline and compensation in perspective. For example, a group that views the number of unproductive, unreasonable searches as small may not show much concern for questions of discipline or compensation, whereas a group that sees that number as large may be vitally concerned with improving present procedures. We decided that if the differences within groups were too great to allow group profiles, then combinations would be made of individuals from different groups, to examine whether similarity of profile, rather than of occupation, affects outlook on the exclusionary rule and questions of discipline and compensation.

Figure 3-1 helps us examine the implications of the four different types of search. Figure 3-2 indicates the major steps encountered in dealing with the problem of protecting Fourth Amendment rights. The initial question is whether there has been compliance with the Fourth Amendment. If there has been, the issue is resolved at stage one. If there has not been compliance, then the issues posed at stage two must be addressed. Should the offending officer be disciplined and should the illegally searched person compensated? If either of these questions is answered in the affirmative, it must be decided when such action should be taken, for or against whom, and how (stage three).

In the first type of search, conducted in accordance with the Fourth Amendment and producing contraband or incriminating evidence, the question of compliance posed at stage one is answered affirmatively and no further question arises. There is no offending officer to consider disciplining and no illegally searched person to compensate.

In the second type of search, also conducted in accordance with the Fourth Amendment, but producing no contraband or incriminating evidence, there is, likewise, compliance, and no need for further questions. An ancillary problem must be noted, however—the possible arousal of citizen and community resentment as a result of frequent invasion of privacy by the police. This resentment is likely to be greater when the search is unproductive, and may indicate dissatisfaction with a wide definition of the term "reasonable."

The third type of search is one that is conducted in violation of the Fourth Amendment that reveals contraband or incriminating evidence. At present the exclusionary rule is the main vehicle both for compensating[1] the individual who has been unreasonably searched and for disciplining the police officer who has conducted the unreasonable search. The immediate questions are first whether the police officer is in any sense disciplined by the exclusion of evidence, and

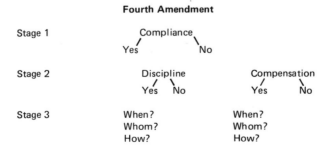

Figure 3-2. Major Concerns in Protecting Fourth Amendment Rights

second whether the exclusion of evidence is an appropriate means for compensating an individual who has been unreasonably searched. Additional questions concern the force of the judicial integrity rationale as an argument for maintaining the exclusionary rule, and the potential effect of proposed modifications of the rule.

Alternative methods of compensation consist of tort and other civil actions, and proposed administrative compensation boards. The attitudes of police officers, defense, and prosecution attorneys toward these alternatives are examined here, and comparisons are made between and within these groups. With respect to discipline, an evaluation is undertaken of attitudes toward criminal prosecution, internal police review, and civilian review.

The fourth type of search, conducted in violation of the Fourth Amendment, produces neither contraband nor incriminating evidence. The main modes of compensation in these cases are again, tort and other civil actions, and proposed administrative compensation boards; the main methods of discipline are criminal prosecution, internal police review, and civilian review. Attitudes of police officers, defense, and prosecution officials are again examined and compared. An important question is whether there is support for, or refutation of, the hypothesis that searches of this type are considered more deserving of compensatory and disciplinary action than unreasonable searches that reveal contraband or incriminating evidence.

Note

1. Though this is an effect of the exclusionary rule, the Court stated in *U.S.* v. *Calandra* 414 U.S. 338, 347 (1974) that this effect is not one of the rule's objectives: "The purpose of the exclusionary rule is not to redress the injury to the privacy of the search victim: '(T)he ruptured privacy of the victims' homes and effects cannot be restored. Reparation comes too late.' *Linkletter* v. *Walker* 381 U.S. 618, 637 (1965)." For an opinion stating that one of the exclusionary rule's functions is compensatory, note the commentary to American Law Institute. *A Model Code of Pre-Arraignment Procedure: Proposed Official Draft* (Philadelphia: The American Law Institute, 1975), Sec. 150.3 where reference is made to the "important, but seldom stated, remedial function to the rule: simply the notion that persons whose rights have been violated by illegal police conduct should be compensated for that injury in some way."

4 Research Methodology

Sites Used in the Study

The study utilizes samples of police, prosecution and defense officials in two areas of a large northeastern state. Since crime is more heavily concentrated in urban areas, it was considered that urban police forces would have greater and more varied experience than would rural police forces or state police. Since the machinery of criminal justice tends to be located in urban areas, such sites also seemed suitable for samples of both prosecution and defense officials.

The two principal cities chosen differ considerably in total population, population density, ethnic composition, unemployment, and crime rates. City B, whose population of about 460,000 is nearly eight times that of City A, has a population density almost twice as great, and a percentage of blacks about four times as great.[1] Its 1970 unemployment rate was 6.0% as compared with 3.7% for City A.

Crime statistics show that the crime situation was considerably worse in City B than in City A for 1970 and 1973. In 1970 11,811 felonies were reported to the police in City B for a rate of 2,522.2 per 100,000 persons, whereas in City A there were 1,165 felonies reported, for a rate of 1,851.5 per 100,000. Misdemeanors that year numbered 31,636 in City B and 1,897 in City A for rates of 6,836.0 and 3,014.8 per 100,000 respectively.

In 1973 crime in City B remained much worse than that in City A, although many of the details changed. While the number of felonies in City B dropped slightly to 11,602 for a rate of 2,507.0 per 100,000, there was a minimal increase to 1,187 reported felonies in City A for a rate of 1,886.5. Misdemeanors in City B likewise dropped slightly to 29,768 and a rate of 6,432.2, while in City A they increased to 1,984 and a rate of 3,153.1. Both the decrease in reported misdemeanors in City B and the increase in City A may, however, be attributed to the changing pattern of misdemeanor motor offenses.[2]

Samples Chosen for the Study

The samples selected consisted of police officers, defense attorneys and prosecution officials in each area.

City A

The Police. The police department in City A numbers a little more than 130 officers. The commissioner had offered inservice classroom training for the administration of the questionnaire; we hoped to sample all officers who underwent this training. When, however, the training was postponed for some nine months, we decided to work through the platoon structure and sample the sixty or so officers who were on regular patrol in the city, together with the ten officers on the detective squad.

Defense Officials. Since many defense lawyers in City A undertook cases in City C in the adjoining county, and vice-versa, we decided to sample defense lawyers from both cities. Lists of lawyers involved in criminal defense work were obtained from persons employed in the criminal justice system. These persons included defense attorneys, prosecution officials, and officials in each city's public defender's office. The lists were compared, the most frequently mentioned lawyers were selected, and a final sample of thirty-seven defense attorneys was thus obtained. The sample included nine lawyers who worked for the public defenders' offices, neither of which employed attorneys on a full-time basis.

Prosecution Officials. The county district attorney's office has five assistant district attorneys. All were to be sampled. In addition, the fourteen assistant district attorneys from the adjoining county were to be administered questionnaires. This was a direct consequence of deciding to sample defense attorneys in City C, the adjoining county's principal city.

City B

The Police. The police department in City B comprises some 1,430 officers. To obtain a sample of persons who were heavily involved with search and seizure, and would complement the more general sample sought from the police department in City A, we decided to sample specialized units. Those chosen were the narcotics squad, the gambling squad, and the tactical task force. Operating citywide, these units employed approximately twelve, eighteen, and seventy-five officers, respectively.

Defense Officials. City B defense and prosecution officials were consulted for the names of criminal defense lawyers. A list of more than sixty lawyers was obtained. As a cross-check, we examined the names of defense attorneys appearing on the city court completed-cases docket-sheets for the months of November and December 1974, and on the city court backlogged-case printout for September 9, 1974. The addition of any lawyer whose name appeared six or more times on the docket-sheets, or who had ten or more cases listed on the backlog printout increased the sample size by only one. The final sample totalled seventy, including five of the six attorneys from the public defender's office.

Prosecution Officials. The county district attorney's office numbers some fifty-five assistant district attorneys, of whom a dozen work in the city court, seven work in the justices courts, and the rest in the county court. We decided to sample as many of them as possible; questionnaires were, in fact, distributed to a little more than forty district attorneys.

Preliminary Work and Pretesting of the Questionnaire

From the beginning of this study we sought critical input from officials in the field. Consultations were held with police and defense officials in Cities A, B, and C, and with prosecution officials in City B. Some input was also obtained from the state police.

Once an initial questionnaire had been constructed, it was subjected to rigorous and continual reassessment and pretesting. Police, prosecution, and defense officials participated in this ad hoc pretesting. In January 1975 a formal pretest was administered.

Police pretesting took place in a large northeastern city. Working in a unit that operated citywide, a lieutenant administered the questionnaire to twenty-eight officers in different precincts throughout the city. The sample was nonrandom, as an effort was made to obtain a broad variety of officers. The questionnaires were analyzed and trends and difficulties in interpretation were noted. For prosecution officials, questionnaires were mailed to four assistant district attorneys in the same city. In the case of the defense attorneys we decided to deliver the questionnaires in person to obviate some of the problems generally encountered by mail response questionnaires, and City C was chosen as a pretest site because of its easy access for the researcher. At that stage we had not planned to use attorneys from that city in the final administration of the questionnaire. Six questionnaires were personally delivered. Five attorneys responded, and none of the six attorneys were used again in the final sample.

After changes had been made in the questionnaire as a result of the pretests, it was again subjected to further informal pretesting, and critical input was obtained from outside sources. The final form was ready for administration by April 1975.

Administration of the Questionnaire

Administration of the questionnaire began in mid-April, 1975 and was completed by the middle of June. A total of about 340 questionnaires were distributed, of which 208 were returned, for a response rate of approximately 61.2%.[3]

Police officers in both cities distributed the questionnaires. In City B it had been required that questionnaires be distributed by members of the police academy. In City A it had been strongly suggested that the best means of distribution was through platoon commanders and the chief of detectives. The advantage of this method is that if key officers are sympathetic to the research project their rapport with their men can be used to encourage responses. This does, of course, take some control of the project out of the hands of the researcher. It also explains why there is no definitive estimate of the number of questionnaires actually distributed.

The researcher had worked with members of the police academy in City B almost from the start of the project, and had developed personal contact among members of the force; 70 responses were received from a total sample of 105. In City A a close working relationship was developed with one of the platoon commanders, but the same degree of enthusiasm for the research was not forthcoming from other key officers. In this case twenty-eight responses were received from a liberal estimate of sixty to seventy questionnaires administered.

In the district attorneys' offices, office personnel distributed the questionnaires. In City A all five assistant district attorneys responded, as did ten of the thirteen sampled in City C. In City B, where the researcher administered some questionnaires, thirty responses were received from a sample of slightly more than forty.

Most of the questionnaires were hand delivered to the defense attorneys personally by the researcher, who hoped to thus bolster response rates. In Cities A and C, twenty-three out of the thirty-seven attorneys sampled responded, and in City B thirty-six out of sixty-five. Overall, those lawyers who had been seen personally tended to respond more often than those whose questionnaires had either been left in their office or mailed to them.[4] The five attorneys working in the public defender's office in City B had their questionnaires personally administered by an official in the district attorney's office, and responses were received from all five.

The Effect of Area and Background Variables
upon Response

Area. The reason for drawing samples from rather different geographic areas with differing crime patterns was to obtain an indication of the extent to which the results of this research could be generalized. The greater the correspondence between the response patterns from the different areas, the wider the application of the research results. Our sampling procedures led to the hypothesis that there would be little systematic variation between the prosecution and defense samples, but some between the two police samples. The reason for this is that the district attorneys were taken from the county district attorneys' offices, and an attempt was made to obtain either experienced or active criminal defense attorneys from the different areas. With the police, however, different types of officers were sought in the two cities. While active specialized units were sampled in the more crime-ridden City B, a more general sample was chosen in City A.

In fact, no highly significant differences were observed when responses were broken down according to area. The major variation in the responses related to the respondent's occupation, not his location. Only in the police sample was any type of overall trend noted. The officers in the specialized units in City B took what may be termed a more traditional, or more extreme, law enforcement approach than their more generalized counterparts in City A.

Background Variables. Since the major hypothesized variation in response was between occupations, it was important to know how experience or active participation in an occupation affected response. If, for example, the views of experienced or active police officers converged with those of experienced or active defense attorneys, then there would seem to be very strong support for their stance. If, however, as was more likely, their attitudes diverged more strongly, then the effect of occupation upon response would be even more striking.

As it turned out, there were no significant differences found when responses were examined with regard to background variables. Certain interesting trends, however, did emerge. Police officers who had made a greater number of warrantless felony and misdemeanor arrests during the past year, and those who had worked on a gambling squad revealed somewhat stronger law enforcement attitudes. Officers who described their primary work as supervisory and/or administrative were inclined in the opposite direction. Those who had been involved in a greater number of suppression hearings during the past year were seen to be less sympathetic to the courts. District attorneys, meanwhile, who had spent more time in the district attorney's office were likely to have a more law enforcement-oriented approach.

Reliability and Validity

Reliability. A traditional method of obtaining estimates of the internal consistency of questionnaires has been to insert some questions twice at different points and to correlate the answers given to the same question. This method may, however, annoy the persons answering the questionnaire and result in lower response rates. In our questionnaire, a few similar but by no means identical questions were asked. Since the questions were attitudinal, and focused on slightly different aspects of the same issue, perfect or near perfect correlations were not expected, as would have been the case if exactly the same question had been asked twice. If the questionnaire was reliable, however, reasonably strong correlations would exist between responses.

Four items were employed to test the internal consistency of the measuring instrument. The intercorrelations of the four items were examined and strong correlations in the specified direction were found between the different items. When absolute values of the correlations between the four propositions were calculated, the mean correlation in the police sample was .52. It was .57 for district attorneys and .64 for defense attorneys.[5]

To test the stability of the instrument, the police sample in City B (the largest subsample) was randomly split in half. Means were obtained for the fifty-six items that utilized a ten centimeter continuum for response, and the means of one-half of the subsample were used to predict the means of the other half. The correlation obtained was .96.

Validity. A measuring instrument is generally acknowledged to be valid if it accomplishes what it is intended to accomplish. Content validity, which reflects the adequacy with which a specified domain of content is sampled, is said to depend upon "a representative collection of items and 'sensible' methods of test construction," and to "rest mainly on appeals to reason regarding the adequacy with which important content has been sampled and on the adequacy with which the content has been cast in the form of test items."[6] We determined the adequacy of the content validity of our questionnaire by thorough case-law and literature research, and by obtaining significant input from personnel in the field.

Because most of the items in the questionnaire were attitudinal, we considered it desirable to insert a few questions that focused on knowledge. Since the validity of the responses could be examined in the light of external criteria, we felt that the distribution of responses to factual questions would reflect upon the overall validity of the questionnaire.

Respondents were asked:

Please check which of the following cases you have heard of in connection with the law of search and seizure.
a. *Gustafson* v. *Florida*[7]
b. *Chimel* v. *California*[8]
c. *Schifrin* v. *Pennsylvania*
d. *Mapp* v. *Ohio*[9]
e. *Elkins* v. *U.S.*[10]

The list of cases included one (*Mapp*) which everyone would be expected to know, and another (*Schifrin*) which was a "sleeper," or nonexistent case. The results, contained in table 4-1, are instructive. Eighty-eight (93.6%) of the

Table 4-1

Awareness of Supreme Court Decisions on Search and Seizure

	Cases Heard of									
	Gustafson		Chimel		Schifrin		Mapp		Elkins	
	Yes	No	Yes	No	Yes	No	Yes	No	Yes	No
Police										
City A	5 / 19.2%	21 / 80.8%	6 / 23.1%	20 / 76.9%	0	26 / 100%	21 / 80.8%	5 / 19.2%	4 / 15.4%	22 / 84.6%
City B	18 / 26.5%	50 / 73.5%	33 / 48.5%	35 / 51.5%	1 / 1.5%	67 / 98.5%	67 / 98.5%	1 / 1.5%	11 / 16.2%	57 / 83.8%
All	23 / 24.5%	71 / 75.5%	39 / 41.5%	55 / 58.5%	1 / 1.1%	93 / 98.9%	88 / 93.6%	6 / 6.4%	15 / 16.0%	79 / 84.0%
District Attorneys										
Cities A & C	9 / 60.0%	6 / 40.0%	14 / 93.3%	1 / 6.7%	2 / 13.3%	13 / 86.7%	15 / 100%	0	5 / 33.3%	10 / 66.7%
City B	14 / 46.7%	16 / 53.3%	28 / 93.3%	2 / 6.7%	3 / 10.0%	27 / 90.0%	30 / 100%	0	18 / 60.0%	12 / 40.0%
All	23 / 51.1%	22 / 48.9%	42 / 93.3%	3 / 6.7%	5 / 11.1%	40 / 88.9%	45 / 100%	0	23 / 51.1%	22 / 48.9%
Defense Attorneys										
Cities A & C	10 / 43.5%	13 / 56.5%	19 / 82.6%	4 / 17.4%	2 / 8.7%	21 / 91.3%	22 / 95.7%	1 / 4.3%	14 / 60.9%	9 / 39.1%
City B	24 / 58.5%	17 / 41.5%	38 / 92.7%	3 / 7.3%	7 / 17.1%	34 / 82.9%	40 / 97.6%	1 / 3.4%	26 / 63.4%	15 / 36.6%
All	34 / 53.1%	30 / 46.9%	57 / 89.1%	7 / 10.9%	9 / 14.1%	55 / 85.9%	62 / 96.9%	2 / 3.1%	40 / 62.5%	24 / 37.5%

ninety-four police officers had heard of *Mapp,* as had all forty-five district attorneys and sixty-two (96.9%) of the sixty-four defense attorneys.[11] In contrast, only one (1.1%) of the ninety-four police officers indicated having heard of *Schifrin,* as did five (11.1%) of the district attorneys and nine (14.1%) of the defense attorneys. All nine defense attorneys, and four of the five district attorneys who claimed awareness of *Schifrin* had checked all five cases.

A second question was: "Do you know of any police officer being criminally prosecuted for an unreasonable search and seizure during the past year?" Since it is widely known that criminal prosecutions for unreasonable search and seizure are rare, and since there apparently had not recently been any well publicized prosecution in either area sampled, it was expected that the number of respondents answering affirmatively would be small. As it turned out, six (6.4%) police officers, two (4.4%) district attorneys, and five (7.8%) defense attorneys said they knew of a police officer being criminally prosecuted for an unreasonable search and seizure during the past year.

A third question was: "Do you know of either a police-civilian or a civilian authority being used at any time in [your state] to review police action?" Since police-civilian and civilian review boards had consistently aroused police opposition, it was expected that officers who knew of such boards would oppose their use, both for issuing and overseeing the enforcement of police rules of conduct. While twenty-nine (30.9%) of the police officers answered that they knew of such a board, none of the eight officers who suggested such a board for issuing, and none of the eleven who supported such a board for overseeing police rules of conduct, claimed such knowledge.[12]

Notes

1. 20.4% as compared with 4.9%.
2. When nonmotor misdemeanors are examined alone it may be seen that in 1973 there was in fact an increase in known misdemeanors in City B, and a decrease in City A:

	Nonmotor Misdemeanors			
	1970		*1973*	
	Number	*Rate per 100,000*	*Number*	*Rate per 100,000*
City A	1,688	2,682.7	1,638	2,603.2
City B	23,197	5,012.5	25,830	5,581.4

3. The estimate of the number of questionnaires distributed is a high one. Probably quite a few less were actually distributed, possibly as few as 300. Of the 208 responses, 1 defense attorney response was received too late for

inclusion in any analysis, and 2 police responses were not included in statistical analysis because of the lack of variation in the answers.

4. Twenty-five (71.4%) of the thirty-five attorneys who had been seen personally responded, whereas replies were received from only twenty-eight (50.9%) of the fifty-five attorneys in whose offices questionnaires were left, and six (50.0%) of the twelve who received a questionnaire by mail.

5. For more detailed information about the four items and their intercorrelations, see appendix A.

6. Jum C. Nunnally, Jr., *Introduction to Psychological Measurement* (New York: McGraw-Hill Book Company, 1970) pp. 136-137.

7. 414 U.S. 260 (1973).

8. 395 U.S. 752 (1969).

9. 367 U.S. 643 (1961).

10. 364 U.S. 206 (1960).

11. The two defense attorneys who did not indicate having heard of *Mapp* did not check off any of the cases and had apparently missed the question.

12. All eight officers who advocated civilian involvement in issuing police rules of conduct also supported citizen participation in overseeing the enforcement of those rules of conduct.

5 Defining the Border of Reasonableness

Introduction

Our theoretical framework suggests the division of searches into a two-by-two table in which the dividing lines represent distinctions between reasonable and unreasonable searches on the one hand, and productive and unproductive searches on the other. In this chapter we will examine the line dividing reasonable and unreasonable searches by comparing the reactions of respondents to certain search and seizure decisions.

Evaluation of the present situation, it may be argued, must precede discussion of modification. We felt that testing reactions to concrete factual situations would provide a basis from which to develop theories of modification that were based on more abstract questioning. Use of actual court decisions as opposed to hypothetical situations allowed the sample responses not only to be compared with each other, but also to be measured against the law in a particular jurisdiction. This comparison showed the extent of agreement or disagreement among the samples and indicated whether respondents were satisfied with the law as it stood or wished to change it.

The data obtained in this part of the research did in fact provide four dimensions of the search and seizure situation. As depicted in figure 5-1 these are (1) respondent's projection of the court's assessment of the reasonableness of the search; (2) respondent's own assessment of the reasonableness of the search; (3) respondent's assessment of the action that would be taken on the street; and (4) the actual judicial decision in the case.

The projected court assessment dimension gives sample projections of the court decisions in the cases. In each case the question asked was, "How likely is it that the courts would consider such a search and seizure reasonable?"[1] A comparison between projected court assessment and the actual court decision shows how accurately respondents projected the court's decision.

The personal assessment dimension provides respondents' subjective evaluations of the cases and a measure of the extent of disagreement that existed among them. Here the question asked was: "Do you personally think that the courts ought to consider such a search and seizure reasonable?" It was expected that the police, representing law enforcement interests, would advocate the widest definition of the term "reasonable," while the defense attorneys, safeguarding civil liberties, would support the narrowest one. The district attorneys, meanwhile, would fall somewhere in between. Active and vigorous

Projected Court Assessment	Personal Assessment
Respondent's projection of the court's assessment of the reasonableness of the search.	Respondent's own assessment of whether the search should be considered reasonable.
Projected Street Action	Judicial Decision
Respondent's assessment of the action that would be taken on the street.	Actual judicial decision in the case.

Figure 5-1. Four Dimensions of the Search and Seizure Situation

participation in an occupation, as manifested by a high involvement in search and seizure matters, might lead to views that represented that occupation's extreme.

In a suppression hearing the court decides between the interests of law enforcement, which advocate the introduction of evidence, and those of civil liberties, which support its inadmissibility on the grounds that there has been an infringement of a suspect's Fourth Amendment rights. Over a large number of cases, the courts would be expected to give some decisions which held evidence admissible and others which ruled it inadmissible. Neither law enforcement nor civil liberties demands would be expected to be fully met. It might be assumed that an equal disagreement with the overall position taken by the courts, manifested by each proponent, is healthy and necessary to a fair and just administration of the laws. As a consequence, if the courts were seen to be leaning significantly in one direction, it might indicate that they are in fact out of touch with the interests of the opposite side.

A comparison between the personal assessment dimension and the projected court assessment dimension indicates the extent to which respondents saw the courts as representing their views, and gives a measure of the respondents' perceived disagreement with the courts. Because of the competing interests of law enforcement and civil liberties, proponents of each may be likely to view the courts as unduly favoring the opposing side, and to support a shift in the balance toward their viewpoint. Thus it might be expected that each group would project that the courts would act somewhat against their interests.

A comparison between personal assessment and the actual court decision reveals the distance between the desired and actual decision in each case. It gives an indication of each group's actual disagreement with the decision, and shows which group, if any, the courts most represented in their decisions. If the courts were seen as unduly favoring either law enforcement or civil liberties interests, then some type of change might be suggested.

Through the use of perceived disagreement with the courts (comparison between personal assessment and projected court assessment) and actual disagreement with the courts (comparison between personal assessment and actual decision), it is possible to determine whether the distance perceived between each group and the courts is accurate. If perceptions are inaccurate, these measures will indicate how an accurate understanding of the court decisions would affect each group's view, and will show whether each group would be more accepting of the courts' position or even more eager for change in the desired direction.

The projected street action dimension, meanwhile, provides a feeling for the on-street action. Here police officers were asked: "Would you have taken action similar to that described above?" Prosecution and defense officials were asked: "How many police officers do you think would have taken action similar to that described?" Particularly important in the police sample was the question of whether projected street action could best be predicted by their own personal assessment of the situation or by their projection of the court's assessment of the case; for if the police were consistently following their own judgment in deciding whether to undertake a search, then the court effect on their behavior would appear to be slight. A second important factor was the frequency with which samples thought such situations occurred. It was possible that the police saw themselves, and were seen by prosecution and defense officials, as being more likely to conduct searches in recurring situations than in situations which seldom arose. If this were so, then guidelines for such situations would be advisable, especially if respondents were also determining the reasonableness of a search on the basis of perceived frequency of occurrence.

Choice of Cases

In order to achieve some form of consistency and to obviate to some extent the problem of respondents knowing the cases, we initially decided to select all the cases from the Supreme Court decisions of a state other than that in which the questionnaires were to be administered. After extensive deliberation and research, five of the six cases were chosen from the decisions of the Supreme Court of a particular northeastern state (State D), while the sixth came from the Supreme Court of State E, where the research was carried out. State D was selected because it presented the best blend of Supreme Court decisions for the purposes of the research project and because its geographical location and characteristics, and its law enforcement problems, are similar to those of State E. Selecting the sixth case from State E, meanwhile, provided insight into the effect of including one case from the state in which respondents worked, and showed whether responses to that case stood out as being markedly different.

Though the courts have often stated their preference for search by warrant,[2] the vast majority of searches are made without a warrant. Search by warrant, implying as it does a period of investigation, differs fundamentally from the warrantless search, which suggests a brief immediate encounter. Moreover, it involves many technical considerations, such as whether the warrant was properly signed, or whether the person or place to be searched, or articles to be seized, were properly described. Because of these factors, we decided not to include searches conducted by warrant among the cases chosen.

The cases selected were intended to represent a series of real situations in which police officers decided to undertake a search on the street. In essence the courts were deciding whether the police officers possessed the requisite evidentiary standard or justification to conduct the search. Since cases involving narcotics, gambling, and weapons offenses feature predominantly in suppression hearings, we decided to obtain examples of each. And since the objective of presenting these cases was to gauge reactions to court decisions and to develop individual and group search and seizure perspectives, we thought it desirable to choose some cases in which the court held the search reasonable and others where it held it unreasonable. A final determinant in selecting cases was whether the facts lent themselves to clear and concise presentation.[3]

In all questions in this section, respondents were given a ten-centimeter line with ends labeled with the opposing viewpoints. Respondents were asked to mark the line at the point which best represented their views. The answers were coded from zero to one hundred, with zero showing the highest possible agreement with the negative side of the question and one hundred the highest possible agreement with the positive side of the question.

In the projected court assessment dimension, for example, the ends of the lines used to answer the question "How likely is it that the courts would consider such a search and seizure reasonable?" were labeled "Certainly would" and "Certainly would not." Thus, a response, or continuum score, of zero indicates a belief that the courts certainly would not consider such a search and seizure reasonable, while a continuum score of twenty shows a belief in the same outcome, but a belief held with a lesser degree of certainty. Conversely, values of one hundred and eighty show similar strengths of belief at the "Certainly would" end of the scale. As the values approach fifty, they show increasingly less strength in the belief indicated. Scores from forty-eight through fifty-two were interpreted as manifesting uncertainty.

In the personal assessment dimension, the ends of the response line to the question "Do you personally think that the courts ought to consider such a search and seizure reasonable?" were labeled "Certainly ought to" and "Certainly ought not to." In the projected street action dimension police officers responding to the question "Would you have taken action similar to that described above?" could place their mark on a continuum ranging from "Certainly would have" to "Certainly would not have." Prosecution and defense responses to the question "How many police officers do you think would have taken action similar to that described?" could range between "All" and "None." In this case, it should be noted, the response was a percentage estimate, and was indeed interpreted as such. A fourth question was: "How often does a situation somewhat similar to this occur?" The ends of the ten-centimeter response line were labeled "Always" and "Never," indicating the perceived frequency of occurrence. Designed to provide differential estimates of the typicality of the cases selected, this question's purpose had been to ensure that atypical situations were not selected, and its omission after formal pretesting had been considered. However, its inclusion in the final questionnaire was felt warranted on the grounds that it would provide a measure of how attitude toward a situation varied in regard to the perceived frequency of such a situation's occurrence. An additional pretest question, designed to explore the problem of respondent knowledge of the cases had revealed a general awareness of the existence of the type of case selected, but no recollection of any specific case.

Respondent Reaction to the Cases

In two of the cases, the evidence discovered was narcotics, in two others it was a weapon, in one it was stolen property, and in the sixth it was policy slips. Two of the cases involved full-blown searches and seizures, two involved "frisks,"[4] and two seizures alone. In three of the cases the Court decided that the action taken was reasonable, in the other three that it was unreasonable. The facts of the cases are given exactly as they were presented to the respondents.

Case One

> The Millcreek Police Department received information that three "Hippies" in a green automobile had been seen placing a package under a snow fence. While two police officers, who had been dispatched to the scene, were searching for the package a man drove by in a red and white automobile. Due to an "unusual look" the man gave the officers as he passed by they gave chase and stopped him. A search of the automobile revealed narcotics.[5]

The Supreme[6] Court of State D, reversing a lower court decision, held by a unanimous 7-0 verdict that the search and seizure was unreasonable. In its holding, the Court stated:

> The only fact upon which the police could rely to establish probable cause was the "unusual look" the appellant gave the police as he drove past them. Such a look, without more, could not establish probable cause for a search.

As can be seen from table 5-1, all samples showed in their projected court assessment a firm belief that the courts would consider such a search unreasonable. The overall police mean continuum score was 22.3, the overall district attorney mean was 10.9, and the overall defense attorney mean was 17.3. In this case, projected court action agreed closely with the actual court decision.

In their personal assessment of the case, both prosecution and defense attorneys overwhelmingly considered the search unreasonable. While the overall mean district attorney continuum score was 8.5, the overall mean defense response was 7.3. On the other hand, the overall mean police continuum score of 45.4 showed only a slight tendency on the part of the police to consider that such a search ought to be held unreasonable. Of the ninety-six police responses, forty (41.7%) personally assessed the search as reasonable and fifty-three (55.2%) as unreasonable.

While defense attorneys were slightly more affirmative in assessing the search as unreasonable than they thought the courts would be, the police were considerably less affirmative in seeing the search as unreasonable, compared with their projections of the court assessment. Thus both police and defense attorneys showed a small tendency to see the courts as somewhat antagonistic to their point of view, with the data showing the police as having the slightly greater justification for their belief. In the police sample, which had the greatest variation both in personal assessment and projected court action, a correlation of .30[7] was observed between these two dimensions, showing a correspondence between a police officer's personal assessment of the situation and his projection of the court assessment. In addition there was a tendency for police officers who saw this sort of situation as occurring more frequently, to be more likely to assess the search as reasonable and to project that the court would determine it reasonable.[8] This tendency was not repeated in either the district attorney or defense attorney samples, and indeed it was this set of correlations in the police sample which showed the strongest association between perceived frequency of occurrence of the situation, and personal assessment and projected court assessment; for while there was an overall tendency in all three samples for perceived frequency of occurrence to be positively associated with both personal assessment and projected court assessment, and while these associations were moderately high in different samples in different cases, the overall effect of perceived frequency of occurrence on either personal assessment or projected court assessment was not significant.

With regard to their projected action on the street, the police were divided in their opinions, recording a mean response of 49.5, with half saying they probably would undertake a search, and half saying that they probably would not. This response compared with an overall prosecution estimate of 47.1%, and an overall defense estimate of 56.7% of police officers who would take similar action. In view of the fact that the Court determined the search unreasonable, these responses show that a substantial number of police officers felt they would

Table 5-1
Summary of Reactions to Case One

			Projected Court Assessment			Personal Assessment					Projected Police Action					Perceived Frequency of Occurrence	
	n^a	$\bar{x}$	s	Reasonable[b]	Uncertain[c]	Unreasonable[d]	$\bar{x}$	s	Reasonable[b]	Uncertain[c]	Unreasonable[d]	$\bar{x}$	s	Would Have Searched[b]	Uncertain[c]	Would Not Have Searched[d]	$\bar{x}$	s
Police																		
City A	28	23.6	33.2	4 / 14.3%	0	24 / 85.7%	42.1	36.2	10 / 35.7%	1 / 3.6%	17 / 60.7%	43.1	40.4	11 / 39.3%	1 / 3.6%	16 / 57.1%	48.5	24.3
City B	68	21.7	26.6	11 / 16.2%	0	57 / 83.8%	46.8	35.2	30 / 44.1%	2 / 3.0%	36 / 52.9%	52.0	36.8	35 / 51.5%	3 / 4.4%	30 / 44.1%	55.3	17.9
All	96	22.3	28.5	15 / 15.6%	0	81 / 84.4%	45.4	35.3	40 / 41.7%	3 / 3.1%	53 / 55.2%	49.5	37.9	46 / 47.9%	4 / 4.2%	46 / 47.9%	53.3	20.1
District Attorneys																		
Cities A & C	15	9.0	6.8	0	0	15 / 100%	7.3	6.1	0	0	15 / 100%	45.7	25.9	—	—	—	39.4	23.4
City B	30	11.9	10.8	0	0	30 / 100%	9.1	9.3	0	0	30 / 100%	47.8	19.8	—	—	—	41.8	17.1
All	45	10.9	9.6	0	0	45 / 100%	8.5	8.3	0	0	45 / 100%	47.1	21.8	—	—	—	41.0	19.3
Defense Attorneys																		
Cities A & C	23	19.4	19.5	1 / 4.3%	0	22 / 95.7%	8.7	19.2	1 / 4.3%	0	22 / 95.7%	58.1	20.6	—	—	—	55.7	18.6
City B	41	16.0	13.6	0	2 / 4.9%	39 / 95.1%	6.5	15.5	1 / 2.4%	0	40 / 97.6%	55.9	20.3	—	—	—	51.6	21.3
All	64	17.3	15.9	1 / 1.6%	2 / 3.1%	61 / 95.3%	7.3	16.8	2 / 3.1%	0	62 / 96.7%	56.7	20.3	—	—	—	53.1	20.3

[a] n varies occasionally by one or two because of missing answers.
[b] Range of scores = 53-100.
[c] Range of scores = 48-52.
[d] Range of scores = 0-47.

be likely to undertake such a search. Responses from both prosecution and defense officials indicated that such a forecast was realistic.

An examination of the interrelationship of the dimensions revealed that a police officer's personal assessment of the situation was far more related to his projected street action than were either his projection of the court assessment or the frequency with which he saw the situation as occurring. Thus while there was a correlation of .75 between personal assessment and projected street action, the correlation between projected court assessment and projected street action was only .39, and that between frequency and projected street action, .35.

A multiple regression run utilizing (1) personal assessment, projected court assessment, and perceived frequency of occurrence as the independent variables; and (2) projected street action as the dependent variable, revealed the latter two variables as explaining only an additional 3.0% of the variation in projected street action to the 56.0% accounted for by personal assessment.[9] The increment obtained by the addition of these variables remained small in all other cases.

When we examined the extent to which the influence of personal assessment on projected street action could be accounted for by projected court action we observed that it was minimal. The original correlation of .75 between personal assessment and projected street action was merely reduced to .72 when projected court assessment was introduced as a controlling variable. In contrast, the correlation of .35 between projected court assessment and projected street action was reduced to .27 when personal assessment was introduced as a controlling variable, thus attesting, in this case at least, to the major influence played by a police officer's personal assessment on his projected street action and the marginal influence of projected court action.

With regard to the prosecution and defense officials, the more often they saw the situation as likely to occur, the more police officers they considered likely to undertake a search. Thus while in the district attorney sample, perceived frequency of occurrence of the situation correlated .51 with projected street action, in the defense attorney sample it correlated .74. In contrast, the correlations between projected court action and projected street action were somewhat smaller, being .19**[a] for district attorneys and .33 for defense attorneys. Thus, for defense and prosecution officials, recurrence of a situation rather than projected court assessment was associated with a police officer's decision to search.

Case Two

> At about 9:20 A.M. police officers received information over their car
> radio that a shooting had occurred and that three males, two blacks in

[a]The significance level has been set at .01. A single asterisk denotes a significance level of less than .01 but at least .05. A double asterisk denotes a significance level of less than .05.

dark clothing and one Puerto Rican in light clothing, believed to be involved, were observed leaving the scene and walking east on Ontario Street. The officers proceeded to cruise the area searching for the three men. About twenty minutes later, they saw a black in dark clothing and a Puerto Rican in light clothing walking together in an easterly direction on Ontario Street about three blocks from the scene of the reported shooting. The officers stopped the men, "frisked" them and discovered a gun.

The Supreme Court of State D, reversing the decision of a lower court, unanimously held (7-0) that the "frisk" was unconstitutional:

At the time of the stopping and the search, B and his companion were merely walking on the street and acting in a normal manner. There was nothing about their persons or in their conduct which would indicate that they were armed or dangerous. The policemen had no reason to connect them with the reported shooting, except that they were walking near the area; that one was a negro and the other was a Puerto Rican, who wore clothing of the general color reportedly being worn by those involved. The policemen had no information of the physical makeup or characteristics of the men they were seeking, and hence, did not know if B and his companion were of the same description. If the policemen were constitutionally justified in searching B under these circumstances, then every Puerto Rican wearing light clothing and walking with a negro in this area could likewise be validly searched. This, we cannot accept.

In their projection of the court assessment, the samples tended to project that the court would determine the "frisk" reasonable, with the police recording an overall mean continuum score of 79.2, the district attorneys one of 77.8, and the defense attorneys one of 78.1. In this case the Court had acted more in the interests of civil libertarians than any of the samples expected them to.

In their personal assessments a similar pattern is to be seen. Table 5-2 shows a solid police assessment of the case as reasonable. The overall police mean continuum score of 92.0 is closely followed by an overall district attorney mean of 82.3. Only the defense attorneys, with an overall mean of 57.9, and 22 (34.4%) of the 64 respondents considering the "frisk" unreasonable, showed much support in their personal assessments for the court decision.

A comparison of overall scores on the personal assessment and projected court assessment dimensions again shows police and defense attorneys registering a perceived disagreement with the court; both again projected the court decision as being somewhat the opposite of what they considered the desired outcome. Though defense attorneys had the greater perceived disagreement, the police had the greater actual disagreement, since the Court decision was the

Table 5-2
Summary of Reactions to Case Two

	n[a]	Projected Court Assessment					Personal Assessment					Projected Police Action					Perceived Frequency of Occurrence	
		$\bar{x}$	s	Reasonable[b]	Uncertain[c]	Unreasonable	$\bar{x}$	s	Reasonable[b]	Uncertain[c]	Unreasonable	$\bar{x}$	s	Would Have Searched[b]	Uncertain[c]	Would Not Have Searched[d]	$\bar{x}$	s
Police																		
City A	28	86.9	20.2	27 96.4%	0	1 3.6%	95.3	5.8	28	0	0	96.0	5.2	28	0	0	70.5	16.0
City B	68	76.1	30.0	57 83.8%	1 1.5%	10 14.7%	90.7	14.7	67 98.5%	0	1 1.5%	92.3	14.2	67 98.5%	0	1 1.5%	69.5	15.9
All	96	79.2	27.7	84 86.5%	1 1.0%	11 12.5%	92.0	12.9	95 99.0%	0	1 1.0%	93.4	12.4	95 99.0%	0	1 1.0%	69.8	15.9
District Attorneys																		
Cities A & C	15	74.3	22.3	13 86.7%	0	2 13.3%	82.2	19.4	13 86.6%	1 6.7%	1 6.7%	86.8	12.2	—	—	—	63.8	24.9
City B	30	79.5	22.9	28 93.3%	0	2 6.7%	82.4	21.4	28 93.3%	0	2 6.7%	88.2	12.0	—	—	—	66.6	19.7
All	45	77.8	22.6	41 91.1%	0	4 8.9%	82.3	20.6	41 91.1%	1 2.2%	3 6.7%	87.7	12.0	—	—	—	65.6	21.4
Defense Attorneys																		
Cities A & C	23	75.2	17.6	20 87.0%	2 8.7%	1 4.3%	57.8	29.1	12 52.2%	2 8.7%	9 39.1%	88.3	13.3	—	—	—	83.0	13.7
City B	41	79.7	14.8	39 95.1%	0	2 4.9%	58.0	28.6	24 58.5%	4 9.8%	13 31.7%	89.8	7.9	—	—	—	77.0	14.2
All	64	78.1	15.9	59 92.2%	2 3.1%	3 4.7%	57.9	28.5	36 56.2%	6 9.4%	22 34.4%	89.3	10.1	—	—	—	79.2	14.3

[a] n varies occasionally by one or two because of missing answers.
[b] Range of scores = 53-100.
[c] Range of scores = 48-52.
[d] Range of scores = 0-47.

opposite of what they both predicted. In all three samples, a significant correlation was noted between personal assessment and projected court action, the correlation being .43 for police, .51 for prosecution, and .58 for defense samples.

In their projections of the action they would have taken on the street, the police, with an overall mean continuum score of 93.4, were almost unanimous in stating that they would have made the "frisk." This compared with a prosecution estimate of 87.7% and a defense estimate of 89.3% of police officers undertaking similar action. These projections of on-the-street action are consistent with the personal assessments and projected court assessments of the case, though in sharp contrast to the actual court decision.

Again, the factor most highly associated with a police officer's decision to search was his personal assessment of the situation. Thus, while personal assessment correlated .56 with projected street action, the correlation between projected court assessment and projected street action was only .22*, and between frequency of occurrence of the situation and projected street action, .13.** When projected court assessment was introduced as a control variable, the correlation between personal assessment and projected street action was merely reduced to .52.

In the district attorney sample, perceived frequency of occurrence and projected court assessment were both fair indicators of police action, with the former variable correlating .32* and the latter, .39 with projected street action. Meanwhile, in the defense attorney sample, frequency was the more influential factor; for while projected court assessment correlated .36, frequency correlated .60 with projected street action.

When background variables were taken into account it was observed that the greater the number of arrests an officer had made during the previous year, the more strongly he was likely to perceive the "frisk" as reasonable, and the more likely he was to state that he himself would have undertaken a "frisk" in the circumstances.[10] Thus a history of aggressive policing seems to relate in this case to a more extreme police view. This trend was not, however, repeated in the other cases.

Case Three

> Uniformed police officers, at about 2:10 A.M., received a report over their car radio that a wig shop had been burglarized. About ten minutes later and about twelve blocks from the address of the reported burglary, they noticed that a man who was walking along the street had a large bulge under his shirt. When the officers pulled close to him he looked at the officers and started to run. Feeling "something was wrong" the officers pursued him. When they apprehended the man they noticed a fresh cut in his right hand. On being asked what was causing the bulge under his shirt, he took out a plastic bag containing three women's wigs which they then seized.

The Supreme Court of State D, affirming a lower court decision, held by a unanimous 7-0 verdict that the seizure was reasonable. In its opinion the Court stated:

> From all the circumstances, the arresting officers had probable cause to believe that B had committed a crime. There had been a burglary reported in the neighborhood. B was concealing something bulky under his clothing. These two circumstances were particularly suspicious coincidences at such an early hour. Added to this, B fled when police officers, easily identifiable as such because they were uniformed and in a squad car, looked closely at him. This certainly indicated a "guilty mind." See *Sibron* v. *State of New York.* . . . Finally B's hand was bleeding. This meshes well with the possibility that he had burglarized a store by smashing a glass window.

Table 5-3 reveals that in their projected court assessment of the case, all the officials were quite firm in their belief that the court would consider such a seizure reasonable. While the overall police mean continuum score was 81.9, the district attorney mean was 82.9 and the defense mean 79.8.

In their personal evaluations of the situation, the individuals sampled also gave a strong assessment of the seizure as reasonable, the police (with a mean continuum score of 92.7) more so than the district attorneys (with a mean of 83.6), and the district attorneys more so than the defense attorneys (who had a mean of 69.4). In this case the different overall mean personal assessments came quite close to each other, with police and defense attorneys registering only a slight degree of perceived disagreement with the projected court decision. Here the correlation between personal assessment and projected court action was .34 for police, .61 for district attorneys and .75 for defense attorneys.

Not surprisingly, the police, with an overall mean continuum score of 92.1, were again almost unanimous in the opinion that they would have taken similar action. This compared to a prosecution estimate of 86.3% and a defense estimate of 89.3% of police officers undertaking such action.

In this case, personal assessment of the situation was highly related to the police officer's projected street action, while frequency of occurrence and projected court assessment were not. Thus, while the police had a correlation of .88 between personal assessment and projected street action, the correlation between frequency and projected street action was .26, and .29 between projected court action and projected street action. When the effect of projected court action on the relationship between personal assessment and projected street action was examined, the correlation was merely reduced to .86, whereas when personal assessment was used as a control variable on the relationship between projected court action and projected street action, that relationship disappeared entirely.[11]

In both prosecution and defense samples, it was perceived frequency of occurrence of the situation which was seen to have the highest correlation with projected street action. Thus while projected court action correlated .08** with

Table 5-3
Summary of Reactions to Case Three

| | | | Projected Court Assessment | | | | Personal Assessment | | | | | Projected Police Action | | | | | Perceived Frequency of Occurrence | |
| | | | | | Rea-son-able[b] | Un-cer-tain[c] | Un-rea-son-abled | | | Rea-son-able[b] | Un-cer-tain[c] | Un-rea-son-abled | | | Would Have Sear-ched[b] | Un-cer-tain[c] | Would Not Have Searched[d] | | |
	n[a]	x̄	s					x̄	s					x̄	s				x̄	s
Police																				
City A	27	84.5	22.5		24 88.9%	2 7.4%	1 3.7%	95.2	6.6	27	0	0	95.4	6.2	27	0	0	64.6	21.9
City B	68	80.8	23.7		60 88.2%	2 2.9%	6 8.9%	91.7	14.0	67 98.5%	0	1 1.5%	90.7	15.0	67 98.5%	0	1 1.5%	66.0	17.2
All	95	81.9	23.3		84 88.4%	4 4.2%	7 7.4%	92.7	12.4	94 98.9%	0	1 1.1%	92.1	13.2	94 98.9%	0	1 1.1%	65.6	18.5
District Attorneys																				
Cities A & C	15	81.7	15.8		14 92.3%	1 6.7%	0	80.3	24.0	12 80.0%	1 6.7%	2 13.3%	92.1	6.4	—	—	—	63.5	22.5
City B	30	83.5	14.6		27 90.0%	2 6.7%	1 3.3%	85.3	13.9	28 93.3%	2 6.7%	0	83.4	16.2	—	—	—	65.7	18.6
All	45	82.9	14.9		41 91.1%	3 6.7%	1 2.2%	83.6	17.7	40 88.9%	3 6.7%	2 4.4%	86.3	14.2	—	—	—	64.9	19.8
Defense Attorneys																				
Cities A & C	23	82.3	17.0		21 91.4%	1 4.3%	1 4.3%	73.0	24.9	20 87.0%	0	3 13.0%	90.4	9.0	—	—	—	82.5	13.7
City B	41	78.4	22.0		35 85.4%	1 2.4%	5 12.2%	67.4	28.7	27 65.8%	4 9.8%	10 24.4%	88.7	11.1	—	—	—	73.0	18.3
All	64	79.8	20.3		56 87.5%	2 3.1%	6 9.4%	69.4	27.3	47 73.4%	4 6.3%	13 20.3%	89.3	10.4	—	—	—	76.4	17.3

[a] n varies occasionally by one or two because of missing answers.
[b] Range of scores = 53-100.
[c] Range of scores = 48-52.
[d] Range of scores = 0-47.

projected street action in the district attorney sample and .15** in the defense attorney sample, frequency correlated .32* with projected street action in the district attorney and .47 in the defense attorney sample.

An examination of background variables as a source of variation revealed that the older a district attorney was, the less strongly he was likely to project that the courts would consider such a seizure reasonable, and the fewer police officers he saw as likely to take the sort of action described.[12] The larger the number of suppression hearings he had handled during the past year, the more likely he was to assess the seizure as reasonable and to project the court assessment as reasonable.[13]

The older a defense attorney was, or the greater the number of suppression hearings he had handled, the less he tended to assess the seizure as reasonable or to project the court assessment as reasonable.[14]

Case Four

> One afternoon, four police officers in an unmarked car observed a man walking along a city street. When the man saw the officers, one of whom he knew to be a narcotics officer, he quickened his pace. The narcotics officer left the car and went after the man, who then began to run. While running, the man threw a cigarette package under a parked car. The officer apprehended the man and recovered the package. It was found to contain heroin.

The Supreme Court of State D, reversing by a 5-1 majority a lower court decision, held that the seizure was unreasonable. The mere fact that the defendant quickened his pace when he saw police observing him from an unmarked police car, and that he broke into a run when an officer left the car and began to pursue him, did not constitute probable cause for his arrest. Since unlawful police action had caused him to throw away the cigarette package, the evidence could not be admitted under either the plain-view doctrine or under the theory that it was abandoned property.

Table 5-4 shows that despite the Court decision, all samples believed quite firmly that the seizure would be considered reasonable. Thus, while the police had an overall mean continuum score of 78.4, the district attorneys returned one of 80.6 and the defense attorneys one of 86.5.

In their personal evaluations of the situation there was also a strong tendency on the part of all persons sampled to consider the seizure reasonable. Again the police, with a mean continuum score of 92.4, gave a stronger assessment of the seizure as reasonable than did the district attorneys, who had an overall mean of 81.9. Defense attorneys, with a mean of 72.0 and 20.7% considering the seizure unreasonable, again gave the least strongly affirmative assessment.

While a comparison of overall mean personal assessment and projected court assessment scores shows both the police and defense attorneys as having a

Table 5-4
Summary of Reactions to Case Four

	n[a]	Projected Court Assessment					Personal Assessment					Projected Police Action					Perceived Frequency of Occurrence	
		x̄	s	Reasonable[b]	Uncertain[c]	Unreasonable[d]	x̄	s	Reasonable[b]	Uncertain[c]	Unreasonable[d]	x̄	s	Would Have Searched[b]	Uncertain[c]	Would Not Have Searched[d]	x̄	s
Police																		
City A	27	82.3	20.4	25 92.6%	1 3.7%	1 3.7%	94.9	6.5	27	0	0	95.3	6.5	27	0	0	64.1	27.1
City B	68	76.8	27.1	57 85.1%	2 2.9%	8 12.0%	91.4	14.7	66 97.1%	0	2 2.9%	90.1	15.3	66 97.1%	0	2 2.9%	65.3	21.5
All	95	78.4	25.4	82 87.2%	3 3.2%	9 9.6%	92.4	13.0	93 97.9%	0	2 2.1%	91.6	13.6	93 97.9%	0	2 2.1%	65.0	23.0
District Attorneys																		
Cities A & C	15	84.3	21.5	14 92.3%	0	1 6.7%	85.8	11.7	14 92.3%	1 6.7%	0	84.2	17.0	—	—	—	68.1	21.9
City B	30	78.8	26.2	27 90.0%	0	3 10.0%	79.9	23.1	26 86.7%	1 3.3%	3 10.0%	80.1	18.6	—	—	—	64.5	22.5
All	45	80.6	24.6	41 91.1%	0	4 8.9%	81.9	20.1	40 88.9%	2 4.4%	3 6.7%	81.5	18.0	—	—	—	65.8	22.1
Defense Attorneys																		
Cities A & C	23	87.8	11.7	23	0	0	71.5	31.1	17 74.0%	1 4.3%	5 21.7%	83.8	20.7	—	—	—	75.4	23.0
City B	41	85.8	18.1	38 92.7%	2 4.9%	1 2.4%	72.4	29.9	29 72.5%	3 7.5%	8 20.0%	85.6	16.3	—	—	—	78.6	19.2
All	64	86.5	16.1	61 95.3%	2 3.1%	1 1.6%	72.0	30.1	46 73.0%	4 6.3%	13 20.7%	85.0	17.9	—	—	—	77.4	20.5

[a] n varies occasionally by one or two because of missing answers.
[b] Range of scores = 53-100.
[c] Range of scores = 48-52.
[d] Range of scores = 0-47.

perceived disagreement with the projected court decision, it is (as was the situation in case two) the police who had the far greater actual disagreement; for the Court not only favored the interests of civil libertarians more than they would have wished, but also more than they projected it would. While defense attorneys had a perceived disagreement in that they saw the court as being more law enforcement-oriented than they would have liked, in actuality they had a real disagreement, if it may be termed such, in that the Court was more liberal than they wanted it. In this case there was a high correlation in all the samples between personal assessment and projected court assessment, with the police registering a correlation coefficient of .52, the district attorneys one of .84, and the defense attorneys one of .74.

Again, the police, with a mean continuum score of 91.6, were almost unanimous in stating that they would have undertaken action similar to that described. This compared with a district attorney projection of 81.5% and a defense attorney projection of 85.0% of police officers taking such action.

In the police sample, both personal assessment and projected court assessment were found to be good predictors of the action the officer said he would undertake on the street. Thus, while personal assessment correlated .86, projected court assessment correlated .60 with projected street action. The introduction of projected court assessment as a control variable on the relationship between personal assessment and projected street action reduced that correlation by only .05 to .81, but use of personal assessment as a control on the relationship between projected court assessment and projected street action decreased that correlation by .24 to .36. Thus as before, it was the police officer's personal assessment of the situation which was most highly related to his decision to search, and not his projection of what the court would decide. Perceived frequency of occurrence of the situation, meanwhile, was only a moderate predictor, correlating .31 with projected street action.

In prosecution and defense attorney samples, projected court assessment was a fairly good indicator of the action they felt would be undertaken on the street, but perception of the frequency of occurrence of the situation was a stronger one. While the correlation between projected court assessment and projected street action was .37 for district attorneys and .44 for defense attorneys, the correlations between frequency and projected street action were .57 and .61, respectively.

When background variables were considered, we noted that, as in case three, older district attorneys were less likely to be strong in their projections of the court assessment of the seizure as reasonable, and saw fewer police officers as likely to undertake the sort of action described.[15] For defense attorneys a correlation of −.33 was found between projected police action and whether the defense attorney had ever been a district attorney. Thus, like older district attorneys, defense attorneys who had previously been district attorneys saw fewer police officers as likely to take the sort of action described.

Case Five

> At about 2:30 P.M. a police officer received information on the police
> radio that a robbery had been committed at a central city location by
> "four or five black males between the ages of seventeen and twenty-one
> in dark clothing" and that the robbers had fled eastward. Moments later
> the officer noticed a man who fit the above description. The man was
> walking very fast six blocks southeast of the scene of the robbery,
> breathing heavily, perspiring and frequently looking over his shoulder.
> The man was stopped. A "frisk" revealed a gun.

The Supreme Court of State D, affirming a lower court decision, held by a
majority of 5-1 that sufficient probable cause existed for an arrest and a
subsequent search.

> Here there is no question that the officers had a reasonable basis for
> believing that a crime had been committed. The issue is whether there
> was sufficient information available at the time of the apprehension to
> reasonably justify a belief that appellant was one of the perpetrators. In
> dealing with probable cause, we deal with probabilities—the factual and
> practical considerations of everyday life (*Brinegar* v. *United States*). In
> this case, the officer had a description of the assailants, albeit an
> extremely general one. He knew the direction of their flight, and the
> fact that they were on foot. Under these circumstances, we conclude
> that he acted reasonably in stopping the appellant six blocks from the
> scene of the robbery because the appellant fit the description given, was
> walking extremely quickly, breathing heavily, perspiring profusely, and
> furtively looking over his shoulder.

Since the Court decided the issue on the existence of probable cause, it did
not have to decide whether a "frisk" was reasonable under the rationale of *Terry*
v. *Ohio* that "a reasonably prudent man in the circumstances would be
warranted in the belief that his safety or that of others was in danger."[16] Since,
however, the evidentiary standard of "reasonable grounds to believe,"[17] (necessary to justify a "frisk,") is lower than the standard of "probable cause"
(required to undertake a full search), and since the nature of the offense[18] could
lead the officer to "reasonably infer that the [defendant] was armed and
dangerous,"[19] it may safely be assumed that on this ground too, the Court
would have found the police officer's action constitutional.

In projecting a court assessment of the case, all the samples felt that it
would uphold the police officer's action. Indeed, as can be seen from table 5-5,
the overall mean continuum scores of the three samples were quite close, with
police registering 71.9, district attorneys 64.2, and defense attorneys 71.1.

In their personal evaluations, the majority also assessed the police officer's
action as reasonable. However, while the police mean continuum score was 84.8,
the prosecution mean was 62.3, and the defense mean 53.9. In terms of percentages

Table 5-5
Summary of Reactions to Case Five

	n[a]	Projected Court Assessment					Personal Assessment					Projected Police Action					Perceived Frequency of Occurrence	
		$\bar{x}$	s	Reasonable[b]	Uncertain[c]	Unreasonable	$\bar{x}$	s	Reasonable[b]	Uncertain[c]	Unreasonable	$\bar{x}$	s	Would Have Searched[b]	Uncertain[c]	Would Not Have Searched[d]	$\bar{x}$	s
Police																		
City A	27	72.7	32.3	20 74.1%	2 7.4%	5 18.5%	86.6	23.4	25 92.6%	0	2 7.4%	86.5	19.9	25 92.6%	1 3.7%	1 3.7%	59.8	22.6
City B	68	71.6	29.6	53 77.9%	3 4.4%	12 17.7%	84.2	23.0	61 89.7%	3 4.4%	4 5.9%	89.3	18.4	66 97.1%	0	2 2.9%	65.4	18.7
All	95	71.9	30.2	73 76.8%	5 5.3%	17 17.9%	84.8	23.0	86 90.5%	3 3.2%	6 6.3%	88.5	18.8	91 95.7%	1 1.1%	3 3.2%	63.8	19.9
District Attorneys																		
Cities A & C	15	63.9	29.2	11 73.3%	1 6.7%	3 20.0%	62.9	32.9	10 66.7%	1 6.7%	4 26.6%	87.7	8.5	—	—	—	67.3	21.5
City B	30	64.3	28.4	21 70.0%	1 3.3%	8 26.7%	62.0	33.1	19 63.3%	2 6.7%	9 30.0%	75.0	23.1	—	—	—	61.5	20.3
All	45	64.2	28.3	32 72.2%	2 4.4%	11 24.4%	62.3	32.7	29 64.4%	3 6.7%	13 28.9%	79.3	20.2	—	—	—	63.5	20.7
Defense Attorneys																		
Cities A & C	22	66.2	26.5	15 63.7%	1 4.5%	6 31.8%	53.9	33.5	11 50.0%	1 4.5%	10 45.5%	84.0	16.2	—	—	—	77.5	17.2
City B	41	73.8	24.4	33 80.5%	1 2.4%	7 17.1%	56.5	32.9	25 61.0%	1 2.4%	15 36.6%	82.5	17.4	—	—	—	72.4	20.7
All	63	71.1	25.2	48 76.2%	2 3.2%	13 20.6%	53.9	33.1	36 57.1%	2 3.2%	25 39.7%	83.0	16.8	—	—	—	74.2	19.6

[a] n varies occasionally by one or two because of missing answers.
[b] Range of scores = 53-100.
[c] Range of scores = 48-52.
[d] Range of scores = 0-47.

assessing the action as reasonable, the police figure was 90.5%, the district attorneys' 64.4%, and the defense attorneys' 57.1%. While police and defense attorneys again manifested a similar degree of perceived disagreement with the court decision that they both predicted, the defense attorneys had the greater actual disagreement, although a majority of them acknowledged that they considered the action reasonable. In this case a high interrelationship between personal assessment and projected court assessment was noted, with the correlation being .71 for police, .91 for district attorneys and .68 for defense attorneys.

As for the action that would be undertaken on the street, ninety-one out of the ninety-five police officers suggested that they would have taken similar action. Their mean continuum score on this dimension was, in fact, 88.5, which compares with a district attorney estimate of 73.3% and a defense attorney estimate of 83.0% of police officers undertaking such action.

In the police sample, both personal assessment and projection of the court assessment of the situation initially appeared to be highly related to the decision to search. Thus, while perceived frequency of occurrence of the situation correlated .32 with projected street action, personal assessment correlated .88, and projected court assessment .65 with projected street action. However, since a high correlation between personal assessment and projected court assessment had been noted, it was again important to find out which of these correlations held strong when the other variable was introduced as a control. As it turned out, the correlation between personal assessment and projected street action dipped slightly to .79 when projected court assessment was introduced as a control variable, whereas the correlation between projected court assessment and projected street action disappeared entirely when the effect of personal assessment on that relationship was examined.[20] Thus again, the major factor associated with a police officer's decision to search was found to be his personal assessment of the situation, and not his feelings of how the court would judge the situation.

In prosecution and defense attorney samples, both perceived frequency of occurrence and projected court assessment were fair predictors of projected street action. Thus, in the district attorney sample, frequency correlated .39, and projected court assessment .42 with projected street action, and in the defense attorney sample the corresponding correlations were .67 and .54, respectively.

Case Six

For more than twenty minutes one afternoon, an experienced police officer, who was an expert on the game of policy, sat in an unmarked car observing an unknown man standing on a city street corner some fifty to sixty feet away. In turn six unknown persons approached the man, each engaging him in a short conversation and then handing him money in bill form. On three of these occasions the man was seen making notations on a slip of paper. The officer could neither overhear the conversations nor see the notations. He arrested the man. A search produced policy slips.

The Supreme Court of State E[21] affirmed the decision of the lower court and unanimously held (7-0) that the search was reasonable. In its opinion the Court stated:

> In the present case an experienced police officer, a conceded expert on the game of policy, who was familiar with its modus operandi, observed the defendant for over twenty minutes and concluded that he was engaged in activities typical of a gambling profession. The officer was warranted in satisfying himself that he had reasonable grounds for believing that a crime was being committed in his presence. (*Jackson* v. *United States*, 302 F.2d 194, 196 [D.C. Cir., 1962]) Here each transaction observed by the officer might have been seemingly innocent, but the repeated pattern amounted to probable cause in the eyes of an arresting officer who was well versed in the behavior of a professional policy operator. Thus under the present law the arresting officer had reasonable grounds for believing that the defendant was committing a crime in his presence and the arrest and incident search were, therefore, proper.

Despite the fact that the Court unanimously held the search reasonable, the projected court assessments of the respondents were quite varied. Table 5-6 reveals that police returned an overall mean continuum score of 51.8, with 43.2% of their number considering that the court would probably find the search unreasonable. Of the district attorneys, who had an overall mean continuum score of 48.8, 44.4% were of this opinion, while for the defense attorneys, who had an overall mean of 60.2, the figure was 24.2%. Considering that this case was taken from a decision of the highest court of the state in which the questionnaires were administered, the high percentage of respondents who projected that the court decision would be the opposite of what it actually was is significant. Indeed, only a few of those sampled indicated knowledge of the case (one member of a gambling squad actually cited it by name).

In their personal evaluation of the situation, the police were quite firm in assessing the search as reasonable, while both prosecution and defense officials were inclined to assess it as unreasonable. Thus, the police showed an overall mean continuum score of 83.1, with only 10.5% considering the search unreasonable; the district attorney mean was 48.4, with 51.2% finding it unreasonable; and the defense attorney mean was 36.9 with 58.0% of them holding the search unreasonable.

In this case, police and defense attorneys had a considerable perceived disagreement with the decision they projected the court would render. However, since the Court held the search reasonable, it was the defense attorneys who had the actual disagreement with the decision. Interestingly, the district attorneys also had an actual disagreement with the decision, since a majority of them personally assessed the action as unreasonable. However, the more often they

Table 5-6
Summary of Reactions to Case Six

	n[a]	x̄	s	Projected Court Assessment			x̄	s	Personal Assessment			x̄	s	Projected Police Action			Perceived Frequency of Occurrence	
				Reasonable[b]	Uncertain[c]	Unreasonable			Reasonable[b]	Uncertain[c]	Unreasonable			Would Have Searched[b]	Uncertain[c]	Would Not Have Searched[d]	x̄	s
Police																		
City A	27	55.0	32.5	16 59.3%	0	11 40.7%	73.5	31.0	21 77.8%	0	6 22.2%	63.0	35.0	17 73.0%	1 3.7%	9 33.3%	52.1	30.3
City B	68	50.6	34.5	33 48.5%	5 7.4%	30 44.1%	86.9	19.1	64 94.1%	0	4 5.9%	84.5	19.0	62 91.2%	4 5.9%	2 2.9%	66.1	19.8
All	95	51.8	33.9	49 51.6%	5 5.2%	41 43.2%	83.1	23.7	85 89.5%	0	10 10.5%	78.4	26.3	79 83.2%	5 5.2%	11 11.6%	62.2	23.9
District Attorneys																		
Cities A & C	15	49.3	31.2	8 53.3%	0	7 46.7%	47.3	35.5	7 46.7%	0	8 53.3%	64.5	21.8	—	—	—	50.9	22.2
City B	30	48.5	29.7	13 43.3%	4 13.3%	13 43.3%	48.9	30.5	13 43.3%	2 6.7%	15 50.0%	62.8	20.5	—	—	—	51.5	19.6
All	45	48.8	29.8	21 46.7%	4 8.9%	20 44.4%	48.4	31.9	20 44.4%	2 4.4%	23 51.2%	63.4	20.7	—	—	—	51.3	20.3
Defense Attorneys																		
Cities A & C	22	64.2	26.5	17 77.3%	0	5 22.7%	47.8	35.5	12 54.5%	0	10 45.5%	73.6	20.4	—	—	—	63.1	27.7
City B	40	58.0	26.5	27 67.5%	3 7.5%	10 25.0%	31.0	28.1	10 25.0%	4 10.0%	26 65.0%	71.1	22.5	—	—	—	67.0	19.8
All	62	60.2	26.5	44 71.0%	3 4.8%	15 24.2%	36.9	31.7	22 35.5%	4 6.5%	36 58.0%	72.0	21.6	—	—	—	65.6	22.8

[a] n varies occasionally by one or two because of missing answers.
[b] Range of scores = 53-100.
[c] Range of scores = 48-52.
[d] Range of scores = 0-47.

perceived this sort of situation as happening, the less they apparently disagreed with the decision, since perceived frequency of occurrence correlated .48 with personal assessment. In the police sample, a moderate relationship was observed between personal assessment and projected court assessment, while in both prosecution and defense samples, it was quite strong.[22]

In this situation 83.2% of the police indicated that they would have been inclined to make a search. Their overall mean continuum score was 78.4, which compares with a district attorney projection of 63.4%, and a defense attorney projection of 72.0% of police officers undertaking similar action. Thus, both prosecution and defense officials appear to support the police feeling that many of them would conduct a search despite their projection that the court would consider the search unreasonable.

Not surprisingly, the factor most related to an officer's decision to conduct a search was again his personal assessment of the situation. While perceived frequency of occurrence correlated .21* with projected street action, projected court assessment correlated .49 and personal assessment .72. When the possible intervening effect of projected court assessment on the relationship between personal assessment and projected street action was investigated, the correlation decreased slightly to .66, whereas the introduction of personal assessment as a control variable on the relationship between projected court action and projected street action reduced that correlation to .34.

In prosecution and defense samples, perceived frequency of occurrence and projected court action were seen as fairly good indicators of the action that would be undertaken on the street, with frequency correlating .44 and .59, and projected court action .55 and .44 with projected street action in the respective samples.

An examination of background variables revealed that while older district attorneys were more likely to project the court assessment as unreasonable,[23] older defense attorneys were more likely to project the assessment as reasonable.[24]

Overall Findings

The six situations chosen represent a well balanced mixture of cases in which the Courts made decisions supporting the interests of law enforcement on one hand and civil liberties on the other. Since the Courts decided in three of the cases that the actions were constitutional, and in the other three unconstitutional; and since each pair of cases included two unanimous decisions and one decided by a 5-1 margin, the Courts can be given a total Court score at the midpoint of the continuum whose extremes represent the interests of law enforcement and of civil liberties.

The sum of an individual's personal assessment and projected court assessment scores on the six cases could range from zero to 600. Since a score of zero represents a view or prediction which shows total support for civil libertarian interests, and a score of 600 manifests total support for law enforcement interests, the courts might fairly be ascribed a score of 300 on these two dimensions. An individual's summed projected court assessment indicates the extent to which he sees the courts as oriented toward either civil libertarian or law enforcement interests. Comparing this score with the total Court score of 300 gives a measure of the accuracy with which the Court stance is perceived. This is important because there must be an accurate perception of the state of the law before the law can influence conduct. An individual's summed personal assessment score (reasonable score), meanwhile, shows the extent to which that individual is oriented toward civil liberties or law enforcement. While a comparison of summed personal assessment and projected court assessment scores indicates the degree of perceived disagreement with the courts, a comparison of summed personal assessment with the total Court score of 300 gives a measure of actual disagreement with court decisions.

When individual projected court assessment scores were summed, we found that the police returned an overall mean of 385.8, the district attorneys one of 365.2, and the defense attorneys one of 391.8. (See table 5-7.) Thus in their overall assessments, all samples predicted that the courts would be more law enforcement oriented than they actually were.

When individual personal assessment scores were summed, the overall mean police score was 490.8, the district attorneys' 366.9 and the defense attorneys' 298.0. As had been hypothesized, the police gave more affirmative personal assessments of the searches as reasonable than the district attorneys, who in turn

Table 5-7
Summed Projected Court Assessment and Personal Assessment Scores

	Summed Projected Court Assessment			Summed Personal Assessment		
	n	$\bar{x}$	s	n	$\bar{x}$	s
Police						
City A	27	405.1	103.8	27	488.9	64.6
City B	67	378.0	95.8	68	491.6	72.6
All	94	385.8	98.3	95	490.8	70.1
District Attorneys						
Cities A and C	15	362.5	56.5	15	365.8	65.6
City B	30	366.5	79.5	30	367.5	76.9
All	45	365.2	72.0	45	366.9	72.6
Defense Attorneys						
Cities A and C	22	395.1	69.4	22	307.4	115.5
City B	40	390.1	64.1	39	292.7	94.2
All	62	391.9	65.5	61	298.0	101.7

were more affirmative than the defense attorneys. Thus, as had been expected, the interests of law enforcement were supported to the greatest degree by the police, and the interests of civil liberties by the defense attorneys.

When these summed personal assessment scores were compared with the mean summed projected court assessment scores, we found that the district attorney scores were almost identical, but the police mean summed projected court assessment score was about one hundred points lower, and the defense attorneys one about one hundred points higher than their respective mean summed personal assessment scores. Thus, police and defense attorneys manifested an equivalent degree of perceived disagreement with the courts, with the police projecting the courts as being more civil liberties oriented, and the defense attorneys believing them to be more law enforcement oriented than they would have wished. This sentiment could indicate a basic dissatisfaction with the court process or merely a recognition of the fact that in seeking to strike a balance between two opposing interests, the courts have to give some credence to the other side's point of view.

Evidence of some dissatisfaction with the court process may, however, be seen in the defense attorney sample, in view of the mean response of 62.8 ($s = 22.0$) to the question of whether "Court decisions on the reasonableness of a search depend more on the judge than on the actual facts of the case." The overall police response of 50.9 ($s = 31.4$) to this question may be taken as an indication that they feel that judges are at least uniform in being somewhat too civil liberties oriented. The district attorneys, whose overall mean personal assessments and projected court assessments were almost identical, alone showed faith in the court process by returning a mean score of 38.5 ($s = 23.8$).

In all cases there was a fairly strong association between personal assessment and projected court assessment. (See table 5-8.) Perceived frequency of occur-

Table 5-8
Association between Personal Assessment and Projected Court Assessment

	Police	District Attorneys	Defense Attorneys
Case 1	.30[a]	.23	.09[**]
Case 2	.43	.51	.58
Case 3	.34	.61	.75
Case 4	.52	.84	.74
Case 5	.71	.91	.68
Case 6	.38	.79	.67
$\bar{x}$	.45	.65	.59
n[b]	96	45	64

[a]Significance level is .01 unless otherwise indicated: * denotes a significance level of less than .01 but at least .05; ** denotes a significance level of less than .05.

[b]The n is subject to minor deviations because of missing cases.

rence of the situation did not, however, have much overall effect on either of these dimensions (table 5-9). Thus, while respondents gave similar personal and projected court assessments, they did not, to any great extent, personally give or see the courts as giving a stronger assessment of the situation as reasonable, simply because they perceived it as occurring more frequently.

While the police and defense attorneys manifested equal perceived disagreement with the courts, the police had the actual disagreement with the balance struck between the interests of law enforcement and civil liberties. Since the cases represented equally balanced decisions on either side, it might be hypothesized that if the court decisions were judged by respondents to manifest a true compromise between these interests, then the total overall mean police and defense official scores on the personal assessment dimension would lie somewhat equidistant on either side of the court mean of 300, with the district attorney total overall mean score falling somewhere between the two of them. However, when these scores were summed, the total overall mean police score was 490.8, the defense attorney mean score was 298.0 and the district attorney mean score 366.9. Thus, in these cases it may be concluded that the courts struck the balance between law enforcement and civil liberties significantly toward the end of civil liberties.

In their projections of the action they would undertake on the street, the police showed themselves to be very much search-oriented. In cases two, three, four, and five they strongly indicated that they would be highly likely to undertake action similar to that described. In case six there was a fairly strong indication that they would search. In case one the attitude was mixed. Prosecution and defense official projections of the percentage of police officers

Table 5-9
Association between Perceived Frequency of Occurrence of the Situation and Both Projected Court Assessment and Personal Assessment

	Frequency/Projected Court Assessment			Frequency/Personal Assessment		
	Police	District Attorneys	Defense Attorneys	Police	District Attorneys	Defense Attorneys
Case 1	.39[a]	.14**	−.01**	.44	−.12**	.22
Case 2	.10**	.36	.23*	.19*	.24**	.04**
Case 3	.20*	.27*	.10**	.25	.32*	.00**
Case 4	.15**	.10**	.26*	.29	.12**	.06**
Case 5	.29	.20**	.43	.27	.11**	.19**
Case 6	.13**	.36	.34	.23*	.48	.17**
$\bar{x}$	.21	.24	.23	.28	.19	.11
n^b	95	44	64	95	44	64

[a]Significance level is .01 unless otherwise indicated: * denotes a significance level of less than .01 but at least .05; ** denotes a significance level of less than .05.

$^b n$ is subject to minor deviations because of missing cases.

who would undertake action similar to that described parallelled the police projections, with cases two, three, four, and five producing the highest estimates, case one the lowest, and case six the next lowest.[25]

The factor most highly related to a police officer's decision to conduct a search was found to be his personal assessment of the situation as opposed to his projection of the court assessment or the frequency with which he saw the situation as occurring. Thus, as can be seen from table 5-10, the average correlation between perceived frequency of occurrence of the situation and projected street action was .26, that between projected court action and projected street action was .44, and that between personal assessment and projected street action .78. The effect of projected court action, as an intervening variable, on the association between personal assessment and projected street action was minimal in each case. However, the correlation between projected court action and projected street action was significantly reduced when personal assessment was introduced as a control variable. Thus, in deciding what action to take on the street, a police officer appears far more likely to follow his own assessment of the situation than to try to second-guess what the courts would decide.

Although projected court assessment was, in prosecution and defense samples, a fair predictor of the action they thought would be undertaken on the street, perceived frequency of occurrence of the situation was a stronger one. While the average correlation between projected court assessment and projected street action was .33 for district attorneys and .38 for defense attorneys, the average correlation between frequency and projected street action was .43 and .62, respectively. (See table 5-11.) Thus the more often they perceived a situation as occurring, the more police officers they considered likely to conduct searches, a finding which appears to highlight the need for police directives for dealing with recurring situations.

When responses were examined as they related to background variables, we observed that long or active participation in a particular occupation led, on certain occasions, to a perspective which closely represented the expected stereotype of that occupation. When composite scores of the dimensions were examined in this fashion, similar findings were noted.[26] Though slight, these trends reemphasize the effect of occupation upon response.

Conclusion

By presenting respondents with six court decisions which were evenly balanced on the sides of law enforcement and civil liberties, we sought an evaluation of the extent to which those sampled felt the courts were striking a fair balance between the interests of law enforcement and civil liberties.

It had been hypothesized that a fair and just administration of the laws

Table 5-10
Factors Related to a Police Officer's Decision to Search

	Projected Court Assessment/Projected Street Action	Personal Assessment/Projected Street Action	Frequency/Projected Street Action	Projected Court Assessment/Projected Street Action Controlling for Personal Assessment	Personal Assessment/Projected Street Action Controlling for Projected Court Assessment
Case 1	.39[a]	.75	.35	.27	.72
Case 2	.22*	.56	.13**	−.02**	.52
Case 3	.29	.88	.26	−.02**	.86
Case 4	.60	.86	.31	.36	.81
Case 5	.65	.88	.32	.07**	.79
Case 6	.49	.72	.21*	.34	.66
$\bar{x}$	.44	.78	.26	.17	.73

Note: n = 96 with minor deviations because of missing cases.

[a]Significance level is .01 unless otherwise indicated: * denotes a significance level of less than .01 but at least .05; ** denotes a significance level of less than .05.

Table 5-11
Factors Related to a Police Officer's Decision to Search: Prosecution and Defense Official Perceptions

	Projected Court Assessment/ Projected Street Action		Frequency/ Projected Street Action	
	District Attorneys	Defense Attorneys	District Attorneys	Defense Attorneys
Case 1	.19**[a]	.33	.51	.74
Case 2	.39	.36	.32*	.60
Case 3	.08**	.15**	.32*	.47
Case 4	.37	.44	.57	.61
Case 5	.42	.54	.39	.68
Case 6	.55	.44	.44	.59
$\bar{x}$	.33	.38	.43	.62
n[b]	44	64	44	64

[a]Significance level is .01 unless otherwise indicated: * denotes a significance level of less than .01 but at least .05; ** denotes a significance level of less than .05.

[b]n is subject to minor deviations because of missing cases.

would lead to a somewhat equal disagreement on the part of police officers and defense attorneys with the overall position of the courts. This hypothesis held true in terms of perceived disagreement. Since, however, the measure of perceived disagreement was based on projected court assessments, and since in their projected court assessments all the samples predicted that the courts would be more law enforcement oriented than they were, this hypothesis did not hold true with regard to actual disagreement with the court decisions in the cases. When a measure of actual disagreement was obtained, it was seen that the police had the actual disagreement with the courts, who were striking the balance between law enforcement and civil liberties significantly at the end of civil liberties. Depending upon the results of broader investigation, the implication of these findings is that it might be desirable to reorganize the administration of the law so that the interests of law enforcement might be more fairly served. Since defense attorneys were no more civil liberties oriented than the courts, and thus the courts would seem to be unduly representing their point of view, it appears that, in the interest of fair and just administration of the law, defense attorneys should consider allowing for such a change.

The discrepancy between projected court assessment and the actual court decision indicates a lack of communication between courts and officials, with a consequent need for clearer decisions and further training and education. The tendency of the police to associate their own personal assessment of the situation with the decision of whether to undertake a search, coupled with the perception of a greater likelihood of police action in recurring situations, suggests a need for police training both in the letter and spirit of the law, especially with regard to frequently recurring situations.

Notes

1. Where required, the terminology is modified to read either "seizure" or "frisk" for "search and seizure."

2. See, e.g., *Camara* v. *Municipal Court* 387 U.S. 523, 528-529 (1967); *McDonald* v. *U.S.* 335 U.S. 451, 453 (1948); *Johnson* v. *U.S.* 333 U.S. 10, 14 (1948).

3. The need for a concise and unambiguous but detailed presentation of all relevant facts was heavily indicated by early pretesting.

4. A lesser degree of search involving a patdown of outer clothing to discover weapons. See *Terry* v. *Ohio* 392 U.S. 1 (1968) and the discussion on case five.

5. In order to preserve the anonymity of the officials sampled the citations of the cases will be omitted.

6. "Supreme" is used to denote the highest court in the state, irrespective of what that court is actually called.

7. The number of responses is given in the table for the particular case under consideration. Because of missing responses, the number may occasionally deviate slightly from the number given. The significance level has been set at .01. A single asterisk denotes a significance level of less than .01 but at least .05. A double asterisk denotes a significance level of less than .05.

8. The correlation between perceived frequency of occurrence of the situation and personal assessment was .44; that between frequency and projected court assessment, .39.

9.

Dependent Variable: Projected Street Action

Independent Variables	Multiple-r	r-Square	Simple-r
Personal assessment	.75	.56	.75
Projected court assessment	.77	.59	.39
Perceived frequency	.77	.59	.35

10. Number of arrests made during the previous year correlated .32 (n = 89) with personal assessment of the case and .25 (n = 89) with projected street action.

11. The correlation became −.02**.

12. Age correlated −.36 with projected court action and −.37 with projected police action. As may be expected, similar correlations are found with years spent in law practice. The correlations were −.26* between years in law practice and projected court action, and −.30 between years in law practice and projected police action.

13. Number of suppression hearings involved in during the last year correlated .36 with projected court action and .27* with personal assessment of the case.

14. While age correlated −.28* with projected court assessment and −.35 with personal assessment of the case, the number of suppression hearings involved in during the previous year correlated −.41 with personal assessment of the case and −.21* with projected court assessment.

15. The correlations were −.38 between age and projected court action and −.36 between age and projected police action.

16. 392 U.S. 1, 27 (1968).

17. 392 U.S. 1, 30 (1968).

18. The offense was armed robbery. A man had been killed during the commission of this crime.

19. *Sibron* v. *New York* 392 U.S. 40, 64 (1968).

20. The correlation became .07**.

21. This is the state in which the questionnaires were administered.

22. For the police the correlation was .38, for the district attorneys, .79 and for the defense attorneys, .67.

23. $r = −.37$.

24. $r = .30$.

25. An interesting trend is the consistently higher estimate given by defense officials, especially in cases where the search is more likely to be considered unconstitutional.

Estimates of the Percentage of Police Officers Who
Would Have Taken Action Similar to That Described

	District Attorneys			Defense Attorneys		
	n	$\bar{x}$	s	n	$\bar{x}$	s
Case 1	45	47.1	21.8	64	56.7	20.3
Case 2	44	87.7	12.0	64	89.3	10.1
Case 3	44	86.3	14.2	64	89.3	10.4
Case 4	45	81.5	18.0	64	85.0	17.9
Case 5	44	79.3	20.2	63	83.0	16.8
Case 6	44	63.4	20.7	62	72.0	21.6

26. It was noted that the more arrests a police officer had made during the past year, the more strongly he felt that the courts ought to consider the searches reasonable, and the more likely he stated he would be to undertake a search ($r = .21*$ [$n = 89$] and .25 [$n = 89$], respectively). In addition police officers who were more involved in suppression hearings projected that the courts were more likely to consider searches unreasonable ($r = −.22*$ [$n = 88$]). Hence, the more active a police officer was, the more law enforcement oriented he tended to be. A similar hardened attitude was found in experienced district attorneys. The older a district attorney was and the longer he had spent in law practice, the more likely he was to project a court assessment of a search as

unreasonable ($r = -.48$ and $-.33$, respectively). In addition, the longer he had spent in the district attorney's office, the more likely he was himself to consider a search reasonable ($r = .28*$). In the defense sample, the more suppression hearings a defense attorney was involved in, the less likely he was to consider a search reasonable ($r = -.26*$ [$n = 60$]), but the more police officers he felt would undertake a search in the given situation ($r = .22*$ [$n = 61$]). Unlike the district attorneys, the longer a defense attorney had spent in law practice the more police officers he saw as likely to undertake searches ($r = .22*$ [$n = 62$]).

6

The Question of Productive and Unproductive Police Searches and the Development of Search and Seizure Perspectives

Introduction

The theoretical framework of the study focuses on the division of searches into those which are legally reasonable or unreasonable, and those which are productive or unproductive. As outlined earlier, this manner of dividing searches gives rise to a two-by-two table in which four types of searches are depicted, consisting of: (a) searches conducted in accordance with the Fourth Amendment that reveal contraband or incriminating evidence; (b) searches conducted in accordance with the Fourth Amendment that reveal neither contraband nor incriminating evidence; (c) searches conducted in violation of the Fourth Amendment that reveal contraband or incriminating evidence; and (d) searches conducted in violation of the Fourth Amendment that reveal neither contraband nor incriminating evidence.

In chapter five we examined respondent reactions to the line the courts drew in six selected cases between reasonable and unreasonable searches, and obtained, through the personal assessment dimension, their own evaluations of the reasonableness of searches. In this chapter we will examine respondent evaluations of the present search and seizure situation by investigating their perceptions of the percentage of police searches which uncover neither contraband nor incriminating evidence. When this has been done, respondent estimates of productive and unproductive police searches will be combined with the summed personal assessment scores obtained in chapter five so that profiles may be drawn up on individual views of warrantless search and seizure, and composite group perspectives may be constructed.

The development of these search and seizure perspectives was considered important because views on the exclusionary rule and its alternatives might be affected by a respondent's perception of the search and seizure situation. Thus, for example, if an individual viewed the population of unproductive unreasonable searches as small, he might not show much concern for questions of discipline or compensation, whereas if he saw that population as quite large, he might be more concerned with improving present procedures.

A vital question that had to be examined before we could begin such an investigation was the nature of the relationship between search and seizure perspective and occupation; for if these related closely, then one variable might be used in place of the other. This was important because, if police perspectives differed from district attorney perspectives, which in turn differed from defense attorney perspectives, then analysis of the data in terms of occupation could continue, though the differences in opinion about the exclusionary rule and its alternatives might not show true differences in attitude, but rather be reflections of differential perceptions of the situation. If, on the other hand, search and seizure perspective did not relate closely to occupation, then combinations would have to be made of individuals from different occupations in order to examine whether profile, rather than occupation, affected outlook on the exclusionary rule and its alternatives.

Productive and Unproductive Police Searches

While our examination of reactions to court decisions focused upon searches conducted without a warrant, we considered it worthwhile to broach the problem of unproductive police searches in terms of searches made both with and without a warrant in order to evaluate whether warrantless searches were more likely to be unproductive than searches conducted with a warrant. Looking at the question in terms of their respective interests, it might be hypothesized that defense attorneys would estimate a larger percentage of unproductive searches than would prosecution officials. The police might be expected to give the lowest estimate of unproductive searches, but this finding could be affected by their ability to make a more realistic appraisal of the situation. In any case, whether or not each group's estimate was realistic, it indicated how large an issue each group saw unproductive police searches to be.

To gauge the percentage of police searches that are seen as conducted without a warrant, respondents were asked to estimate "What percentage of all police searches is made without a warrant?" As can be seen from table 6-1, the mean answers of all the samples were extremely close; all hovered around the 70% mark. This finding supports the general impression that the majority of police searches are carried out without a warrant, though at the same time it seems to indicate significant use of the warrant system.

To obtain estimates of the extent of unproductive police searches, respondents were asked "In your opinion, what percentage of all police searches conducted *with* a warrant produces contraband or incriminating evidence?" The question was repeated for warrantless searches.[1]

Table 6-1 reveals some interesting trends. While prosecution and defense officials saw a marked difference between the success rates of searches conducted with and without a warrant, police officers considered warrantless searches only marginally less successful than those conducted with a warrant.

Table 6-1
Perceptions of Searches Conducted with and without Warrants and of Productive and Unproductive Searches

	% of Searches Conducted Without a Warrant			% of Searches Conducted With a Warrant Which Are Productive			% of Searches Conducted Without a Warrant Which Are Productive			% of Unreasonable Searches Where the Evidence is Essential to Obtain Suspect's Conviction		
	n	x̄	s	n	x̄	s	n	x̄	s	n	x̄	s
Police												
City A	25	69.9	21.7	25	63.8	23.7	25	62.1	21.2	25	57.2	24.1
City B	67	70.7	19.1	67	62.8	25.0	67	56.0	18.4	66	72.8	21.6
All	92	70.5	19.7	92	63.1	24.5	92	57.7	19.2	91	68.5	23.3
District Attorneys												
Cities A & C	14	73.8	15.4	14	81.6	11.1	13	60.0	21.1	14	67.1	17.9
City B	29	70.1	16.7	30	81.0	14.9	29	47.8	24.2	30	74.6	22.5
All	43	71.3	16.2	44	81.2	13.7	42	51.8	23.8	44	72.2	21.2
Defense Attorneys												
Cities A & C	22	71.4	18.7	22	76.7	12.6	22	47.3	21.1	22	73.4	19.4
City B	41	73.0	12.9	40	72.3	14.2	41	36.8	20.3	41	79.3	17.9
All	63	72.4	15.0	62	73.8	13.7	63	40.4	21.0	63	77.2	18.5

Thus, district attorneys saw an average of 81.2% of warrant searches as productive and 51.8% of warrantless searches as productive, and defense attorneys considered the average success rates to be 73.8% and 40.4%, respectively; but police officers saw an average 63.1% of warrant searches and 57.7% of warrantless searches as productive. These figures show that, as hypothesized, defense attorneys saw more warrantless searches as unproductive than did prosecution attorneys, who, in turn, saw more as unproductive than did police officers. With regard to searches conducted with a warrant, however, the police position is inverted, and the relationship became police, then defense attorneys, and then district attorneys seeing a greater percentage of searches as unproductive. This change in relationship may perhaps indicate police dissatisfaction with the warrant system and a correspondingly greater faith in that system on the part of prosecution and defense attorneys. The police dissatisfaction may be well founded. On the other hand it may be the result of a self-serving need to convince themselves and others that it is not worth the trouble to obtain a warrant. Or it may be the result of a selective memory process; for they may clearly remember situations where they went to the trouble of obtaining warrants and were then unsuccessful, or where warrantless searches were successful, but may tend to forget both unsuccessful warrantless searches and successful warrant searches. Whatever the reason for the close police estimates of successful warrant and warrantless searches, the fact remains that they saw over 40% of warrantless searches as unproductive. Thus, all of the samples indicate that the issue of unproductive warrantless searches is one that deserves consideration.

While searches may be unproductive in the sense that they fail to uncover contraband or incriminating evidence, they may also be unproductive in the sense that the evidence seized may not be admissible in court. Indeed, much emphasis has been placed in earlier research (for example, in the works of Oaks[2] and Spiotto[3]) on the relationship between the suppression of evidence and the dismissal of charges against a defendant. To examine this facet of unproductive police searches, respondents were asked to estimate "In what percentage of cases where there has been an 'unreasonable search and seizure' is the illegally seized evidence essential to obtain the suspect's conviction?"

As table 6-1 shows, the police saw such evidence as essential 68.5% of the time, the district attorneys 73.3%, and the defense attorneys 77.2% of the time. Such figures well attest to the significance of the suppression hearing. Interestingly, the greater the number of suppression hearings a police officer had been involved in during the previous year, the greater the percentage of cases in which he perceived the illegally seized evidence as essential for obtaining a conviction.[4] Likewise, officers who had worked on a gambling squad tended to see the introduction of illegally seized evidence as essential in a greater percentage of cases.[5]

Search and Seizure Perspectives

Search and seizure perspectives were obtained by combining an individual's summed personal assessment score with his estimate of productive warrantless police searches. While his summed personal assessment or reasonable score fixed the horizontal plane of his perspective, his productive score fixed the vertical one. To summarize the different types of perspective found among the three samples, the two dimensions were divided into high, medium, and low categories. These findings are presented in figure 6-1, which shows that the distribution patterns of the three samples varied considerably.

While 82.6% of the police officers fell into the high reasonable-high productive and high reasonable-low productive cells, with 29.3% in the former and 53.3% in the latter, 76.7% of the defense attorneys were in the low reasonable-medium productive, medium reasonable-low productive and medium reasonable-medium productive categories, with the percentages being 15.0%, 31.7%, and 30.0%, respectively. The main distribution of the district attorneys, meanwhile, lay between police and defense distributions, with 83.3% of the sample in the medium reasonable-low productive, medium reasonable-medium productive, medium reasonable-high productive and high reasonable-medium productive categories. The figures for these four were 16.7%, 28.6%, 19.0%, and 19.0%, respectively.

While this schema gives a good indication of the dispersion of the samples among the reasonable-productive categories, it also shows that search and seizure perspective does relate to occupation. The numbers in the individual cells are too small to allow meaningful comparison across samples of individuals in the same cells. Moreover, the collapsing of categories would achieve little, since both police and defense attorney samples would end up with most of their number in one category and few in the other. The result was that, since search and seizure perspective did relate to occupation, analysis of the data in terms of occupation should be continued, although it raised the possibility that differences in opinion about the exclusionary rule might not show true differences in attitude, but rather reflect differences in perception of the present situation.

In order to compare the overall search and seizure perspectives of each of the three occupations, composite group profiles were constructed by combining the mean summed personal assessment (reasonable) score and mean productive score for each group. The mean reasonable scores were assumed to represent the average proportion of searches each group considered reasonable. Since summed personal assessment scores could range from zero to 600, with zero representing a view that none of the searches could in any way be considered reasonable, and 600 representing the position that all of the searches were completely reasonable, the group summed personal assessment scores were translated into approximations of the percentage of searches considered reasonable. The mean

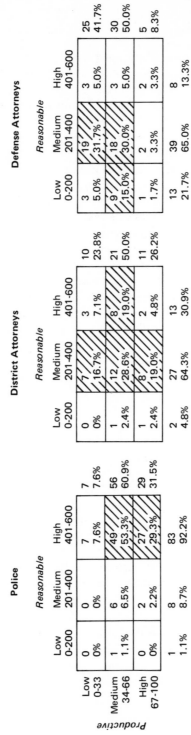

Figure 6-1. Breakdown of Respondents by Search and Seizure Perspective

police summed personal assessment or reasonable score obtained in chapter 5 was, it may be recalled, 490.8, while for district attorneys the figure was 366.9 and for defense attorneys 298.0. These scores were combined with the mean percentage of warrantless searches that officials considered productive, which for the police was 57.7%, for district attorneys 51.6%, and for defense attorneys 40.4%.

Figure 6-2 reveals that the group profiles drawn from these figures differ considerably. While the population of searches which police officials considered both reasonable and productive was very high, averaging some 47.2% of the searches under consideration, the population of searches they considered both unreasonable and unproductive averaged only 7.7%. For district attorneys these figures were 31.6% and 18.8%, while for defense attorneys they were 20.1% and 30.0%, respectively. The percentage of searches which police officials saw as reasonable but unproductive was 34.6% while for both district and defense attorneys this figure was 29.6%. Finally, while police officials saw 10.5% of searches as unreasonable, but productive, district attorneys set this figure at 20.0%, and defense attorneys at 20.3%.

From this it may be seen that both hypothesized relationships were substantiated. Police perceived more searches as reasonable and productive than did district attorneys, who in turn saw more searches as reasonable and productive than did defense attorneys. Conversely, defense attorneys saw more searches as unproductive and unreasonable than did district attorneys, who saw more searches as unreasonable and unproductive than did the police. While the estimated percentage of reasonable unproductive searches averaged much the same for all three samples, district and defense attorneys saw twice as many searches as unreasonable but productive as did the police.

The different group perspectives reemphasize the fact that search and seizure perspectives relate to occupation. This means that when differences of opinion toward the exclusionary rule and its alternatives are examined and variations noted between the occupations, the different perceptions of the respective occupations regarding warrantless search and seizure must be borne in mind. Respondents of differing occupations may disagree because they view the overall situation differently, and not because they see different degrees of merit in the various mechanisms. Moreover, since differences of opinion may relate to varying perceptions, changes in opinion may be accomplished by showing that the actual situation differs from the way it is perceived.

Finally, we sought to determine how different perspectives within an occupation related to opinions about the exclusionary rule and its alternatives. Given that perspectives differed among the samples, the question was whether persons within a sample who had extreme perspectives for that sample also had more extreme opinions on the exclusionary rule and its alternatives. The method decided upon for this analysis was to draw high-low categories around the means of each of the three samples. This was considered the best approach, since the interrelationships of the samples were known, and this method allowed sufficient numbers for comparison.

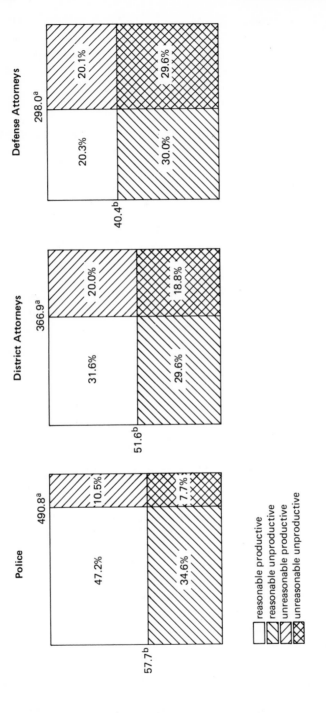

Figure 6-2. Composite Group Search and Seizure Perspectives

Initially each sample was divided into four categories. The means provided a division point for high-low categories on both the reasonable-unreasonable and productive-unproductive dimensions. As a result, high reasonable-high productive, high reasonable-low productive, low reasonable-high productive and low reasonable-low productive categories were obtained for each sample. A fifth category, medium reasonable-medium productive, was added by including all cases located within three-quarters of a standard deviation[6] of both the reasonable and productive dimension means. The resulting categories are depicted in figure 6-3, while a breakdown of the numbers in each category is presented, by sample, in figure 6-4. The mean reasonable and productive scores are also included. The figure shows that the mean low reasonable and mean low productive scores in different categories of the same sample are close. This proximity of means is found also among the mean high scores (with the exception perhaps of the mean high productive police scores), while the distance between the mean high and low scores is significant. Between samples, the relationship of police > district attorneys > defense attorneys holds true with regard to both dimensions, with the sole exception of the productive score of the low reasonable-high productive district attorneys, which is higher than the equivalent mean police score.

Only in the police sample was there any relationship between search and seizure perspective and views on the exclusionary rule and its alternatives. Officers with low reasonable-low productive perspectives tended to disagree considerably with those with high reasonable-high productive perspectives, thus leaving open the possibility that either group might be converted to the other's point of view upon a showing that the warrantless search and seizure situation was not as they perceived it.

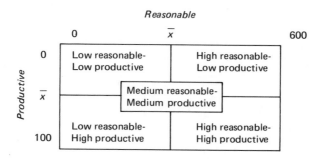

Figure 6-3. Categories of Search and Seizure Perspectives Derived from Group Means

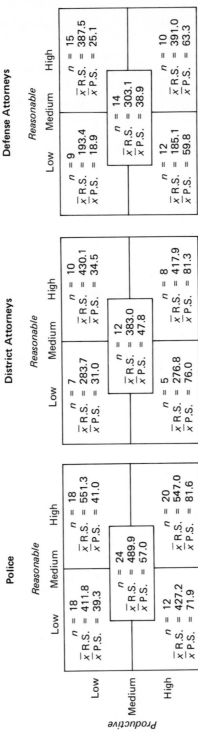

Figure 6-4. Search and Seizure Perspectives Derived from Group Means

Conclusion

In this chapter we examined the question of unproductive police searches, and drew up individual and group perspectives on warrantless search and seizure. While all the samples saw a considerable percentage of warrantless searches as unproductive, the police saw warrant searches as being only marginally more productive. All agreed that most police searches are conducted without a warrant.

Search and seizure perspective related closely with occupation. Hence, if attitudes differed between occupations it could be because perceptions of the situation differed. Within occupations, however, only the police showed attitudes that varied according to search and seizure perspective.

Notes

1. "In your opinion, what percentage of all police searches conducted *without* a warrant produces contraband or incriminating evidence?"

2. Dallin H. Oaks, "Studying the Exclusionary Rule in Search and Seizure," *University of Chicago Law Review* 37 (1970): 737.

3. James E. Spiotto, "Search and Seizure: An Empirical Study of the Exclusionary Rule and its Alternatives," *Journal of Legal Studies* 2 (1973): 247.

4. $r = .36$ ($n = 88$)

5. $r = .25*$ ($n = 60$)

6. Three-quarters of a standard deviation was chosen because it provided the best overall dispersion of respondents among the five categories.

7 The Deterrent, Disciplinary, and Compensatory Functions Performed by the Exclusionary Rule

Introduction

After obtaining overall perceptions of the warrantless search and seizure situation and seeing how composite police, prosecution, and defense perspectives differed, we examined the role played by the exlcusionary rule in protecting Fourth Amendment rights.

Previous research has focused on the drawbacks of the exclusionary rule and intensified the cry for its modification or abolition. Little work, however, has been done to evaluate the positive functions it may fulfill. Since arguments for the retention of the exclusionary rule must be predicated upon a showing of its positive attributes, this is a vital area for investigation.

We examined the three major positive functions the exclusionary rule may be fulfilling: as a deterrent, as a disciplinary mechanism, and as a compensatory mechanism. Strong support for the exclusionary rule's performance in one or more of these roles would argue well for its retention, while negative sentiments would add weight to the side of those who seek either to limit or abolish it.

In chapter two, two theoretical justifications were seen to lie behind the exclusionary rule. The first, termed the judicial integrity or normative rationale, is that the courts should not participate in illegal behavior by admitting the evidence obtained by such behavior. The second, termed the deterrent or factual rationale, is that if the courts excluded evidence which had been illegally seized, police officials would be deterred from violating the Fourth Amendment's prohibition against unreasonable searches and seizures. While the Supreme Court had been observed to focus in earlier cases upon the normative rationale, it had been seen, since its decision in *Mapp*[1] in 1961, to advance the factual rationale. Questions concerning the rule's performance as a deterrent or disciplinary mechanism relate to the factual rationale; and, since compensation is the end product of the normative rationale, questions concerning the rule's compensatory function and the force of the judicial integrity theory relate to the normative rationale.

If support were found for the deterrent effect, it would be expected to come from the police, who would feel they had most cause to complain about the chilling effect of the exclusionary rule upon law enforcement. These officers might also be the most likely to consider the exclusionary rule as a disciplinary mechanism, and the least likely to advocate its use as a compensatory device.

At the other extreme, defense attorneys might be most likely to have strong negative feelings about the deterrent and disciplinary functions of the exclusionary rule, and see the greatest merit in its use as a compensatory device. District attorneys, with similar educational backgrounds to the defense attorneys, and similar law enforcement interests to the police, might be expected to take a middle ground.

To test these three positive attributes of the exclusionary rule, a series of statements was presented to which respondents could indicate scaled agreement or disagreement on a ten-centimeter continuum. Once again a score of 100 indicated the highest possible agreement with the statement, a score of zero the lowest.

Deterrence

In terms of the exclusionary rule, deterrence may be considered to have three components: (1) knowledge of the factors meant to lead to deterrence; (2) conscious thought of those factors at the time when deterrence should occur; and (3) the actual act of deterrence itself.[2] This means that a police officer should be sufficiently knowledgeable in the law to distinguish between situations in which it is legally permissible for him to search and those in which it is not. He must, therefore, know what factors make it illegal for him to search in particular circumstances. Secondly, he must relate this knowledge to the circumstances at the time he is considering a search. Finally, recall of these factors must exert sufficient influence on him to deter him from undertaking an illegal search.

To explore the perceived deterrent effect of the exclusionary rule, respondents were asked to register their scaled agreement or disagreement with the proposition: "The exclusion of illegally seized evidence in court proceedings discourages police officers from making many kinds of searches they would otherwise make" (*General Discouraging Effect of Rule*).[a]

As can be seen from table 7-1, the police as a whole were somewhat inclined to believe that the exclusionary rule discouraged them from making searches they would otherwise undertake. District attorneys and defense lawyers, on the other hand, were inclined to the opposite view. While the overall police mean continuum score was 65.5, the district attorney mean was 42.8, and the defense attorney mean 38.9. Since the question asked about discouragement rather than deterrence, the lack of support for the exclusionary rule's effect is more striking seeing that discouragement is not as strong a term as deterrence. And since the question was about the rule's general discouraging effect, it explored the rule's ability to discourage both legal and illegal searches, leaving open the possibility that the little support the exclusionary rule received might relate to the negative

[a]This phrase is an abbreviated form of the proposition. Such phrases will appear in text and tables throughout the book.

Table 7-1
Deterrent Functions of the Exclusionary Rule

	General Discouraging Effect of Rule			Officer's Concern With Admissibility of Evidence			Officer's Knowledge of the Law		
	n	$\bar{x}$	s	n	$\bar{x}$	s	n	$\bar{x}$	s
Police									
City A	26	61.8	37.6	26	56.5	34.4	26	69.8	27.7
City B	67	67.0	32.8	68	57.0	31.4	68	65.8	25.9
All	93	65.5	34.1	94	56.9	32.1	94	66.9	26.4
District Attorneys									
Cities A and C	15	43.7	33.9	15	44.7	24.3	15	51.4	20.6
City B	30	42.4	26.6	30	35.0	22.4	30	58.1	24.6
All	45	42.8	28.9	45	38.2	23.2	45	55.9	23.3
Defense Attorneys									
Cities A and C	22	48.3	36.7	23	36.1	29.4	22	52.8	17.3
City B	41	33.9	30.2	41	30.4	26.0	41	55.3	28.0
All	63	38.9	33.1	64	32.5	27.2	63	54.4	24.7

aspect of discouraging police officers from undertaking all searches, including legal ones.

A second proposition explored whether the exclusionary rule was a factor police officers considered in deciding whether to undertake a search. The proposition was: "An important factor in a police officer's decision to search is whether the article he is looking for will be admissible as evidence in court" (*Officer's Concern with Admissibility of Evidence*). Reactions to this question paralleled those to the previous question. Police as a whole were slightly less affirmative (their overall mean continuum score was 56.9), and district attorneys and defense attorneys slightly more negative (38.2 and 32.5, respectively). The correlations between the two questions were fairly high in all three samples,[3] indicating that respondents who considered that the exclusionary rule discourages police officers from undertaking searches also believed that police officers tend to think about the admissibility of evidence when deciding whether to undertake a search. A comparison of the means of the two questions, however, indicated that in the police sample, where the mean response to the question of the rule's general discouraging effect was higher, much of the discouraging effect might be negative, in that the police could have been unhappy with the implementation of the exclusionary rule and thus discouraged from making searches in general. This conclusion drew support from both the prosecution and defense samples; while they generally believed that the exclusionary rule did not have a discouraging effect, their even more negative position toward an officer's concern with the admissibility of evidence indicated little support for the theory that the exclusionary rule played a positive deterrent role.

While we had observed that the exclusionary rule had little or no positive deterrent effect on a police officer's decision to search, we had yet to examine whether the purpose of deterrence was perceived to be weakened by an officer's lack of knowledge as to what constitutes a legal search. By focusing on perceptions of the police officer's knowledge of the law, the statement "A police officer usually knows whether a search he is making is legal" (*Officer's Knowledge of the Law*) sought to examine this facet.

Table 7-1 reveals that the police, with a mean continuum score of 66.9, were inclined to believe that police officers usually do know whether searches they are making are legal. However, district and defense attorneys, recording overall means of 55.9 and 54.4, respectively, were somewhat less affirmative. The low means are far from encouraging, especially in view of the qualifying adverb "usually" contained in this question. This lack of support for the belief that police officers are sufficiently knowledgeable in the law to distinguish between situations in which it is legally permissible to search and those in which it is not, is further illustrated by the almost total lack of correlation between *Officer's Knowledge of the Law* and both the *General Discouraging Effect of the Rule* and *Officer's Concern with Admissibility of Evidence*.[4] Thus, respondents who felt that the exclusionary rule tends to discourage police officers from undertaking searches also felt that police officers tend to think about the admissibility of evidence when deciding whether to undertake a search, but were no more likely than other respondents to believe that a police officer usually knows whether a search he is making is legal. The general perception thus seems to be that when a police officer weighs the legality of a search he is about to undertake, he is likely to follow his own subjective assessment of the situation, which may or may not coincide with the court ruling. This perception, it should be noted, supports a similar finding in chapter five.

The conclusion is that not only does the exclusionary rule not deter in most circumstances, but when it does deter, it does so in a negative fashion, and on the basis of limited knowledge of the law. With officers following their own personal assessments of the situation, it appears to police, prosecution, and defense officials that the exclusionary rule is not functioning as a positive deterrent mechanism.

Discipline

While deterrence had been perceived as something of a myth, it remained to be explored whether the exclusionary rule could nevertheless be said to be fulfilling a disciplinary function. Respondents were asked to register their scaled agreement or disagreement with the statements: "The courts punish a police officer by excluding evidence he has illegally seized" (*Rule Punishes*) and "A police officer feels a personal loss when evidence he has seized is excluded in court" (*Officer Feels Personal Loss*).

The former question sought a general estimate of whether a police officer is punished in any way by the fact that evidence he has illegally seized is excluded in court. The latter question explored perceptions of the subjective feelings of deprivation or punishment a police officer may undergo when evidence he has seized is excluded.

Table 7-2 reveals that none of the three samples saw the exclusionary rule as fulfilling a disciplinary function. The district and defense attorneys, who recorded mean continuum scores of 26.0 and 25.2 respectively, were more emphatic in this opinion than were the police, whose overall mean was 39.5. All three, however, thought that a police officer feels a personal loss when evidence he has seized is excluded in court; the police had a mean continuum score of 58.8, and district and defense attorney means were 55.2 and 65.9, respectively. The correlation between the two questions showed that the police tended to equate feelings of personal loss with punishment.[5] For district attorneys, however, this equation was far less strong,[6] and nonexistent for defense officials.[7]

Compensation and the Normative Rationale

While questions concerning the deterrent and disciplinary functions of the exclusionary rule relate to the factual rationale, questions concerning compensation involve the normative rationale. By compensation we mean the redress afforded a wronged individual either by the suppression of the illegally seized evidence or by financial remuneration. At this point we are discussing only the exclusion of evidence; the issue of financial remuneration will be addressed later.

Table 7-2
Disciplinary Functions of the Exclusionary Rule

	Rule Punishes			Officer Feels Personal Loss		
	n	$\bar{x}$	s	n	$\bar{x}$	s
Police						
City A	25	47.1	36.1	26	71.1	30.6
City B	68	36.7	36.7	68	54.0	33.6
All	93	39.5	36.7	94	58.8	33.5
District Attorneys						
Cities A and C	15	19.7	27.7	15	67.3	27.4
City B	30	29.1	28.6	30	49.2	26.1
All	45	26.0	28.3	45	55.2	27.6
Defense Attorneys						
Cities A and C	23	26.3	29.3	23	68.7	23.3
City B	41	24.6	26.3	41	64.3	26.4
All	64	25.2	27.2	64	65.9	25.2

The first two questions focused on support of the normative rationale, and especially perceptions of the propriety of the exclusionary rule as a means of atoning for the infringement of Fourth Amendment rights. Respondents were asked for their scaled agreement or disagreement with the proposition: "A suspect who has been illegally searched should have the illegally seized evidence excluded in court" (*Evidence Should be Excluded*).

Table 7-3 reveals that prosecution and defense officials felt strongly that suspects who have been illegally searched should have the illegally seized evidence excluded in court, but the police were ambivalent about the issue. Thus, while district attorneys recorded a mean continuum score of 77.4, and defense attorneys one of 89.8, the police mean was 49.6.

The second proposition looked at the other side of the issue: "It would be improper for the courts to admit any illegally seized evidence because they would be approving illegal conduct" (*Impropriety of Admitting Evidence*).

The responses, shown in table 7-3, paralleled those on whether evidence should be excluded, though district attorneys, and to a lesser extent defense attorneys, were less strong in their support for this proposition. While the overall district attorney mean continuum score was 65.6, the defense attorney mean was 85.8. The police, with an overall mean of 52.3, were again ambivalent. As might be expected, respondents who thought that illegally seized evidence should be excluded also thought it improper for the courts to admit such evidence. Thus, while there was a correlation of .61 in the police sample between these two questions, in the prosecution sample the correlation was .48, and in the defense sample, .50. In some ways the propriety issue had the greatest weight in the police sample. The strongest correlation between the questions was

Table 7-3
Compensatory Functions of the Exclusionary Rule

	Evidence Should Be Excluded			Impropriety of Admitting Evidence			Suspect Gains Too Much		
	n	$\bar{x}$	s	n	$\bar{x}$	s	n	$\bar{x}$	s
Police									
City A	26	51.7	37.6	25	60.4	30.4	26	61.9	37.0
City B	68	48.8	34.2	66	49.3	32.4	67	81.8	24.5
All	94	49.6	35.0	91	52.3	32.1	93	76.3	29.7
District Attorneys									
Cities A and C	15	73.3	33.0	15	64.3	36.1	15	37.5	33.7
City B	30	79.5	23.2	30	66.3	30.0	30	45.9	33.5
All	45	77.4	26.6	45	65.6	31.8	45	43.1	33.4
Defense Attorneys									
Cities A and C	23	89.5	21.6	23	87.4	22.1	23	12.0	21.2
City B	41	89.9	20.5	41	84.8	24.7	41	19.3	28.4
All	64	89.8	20.7	64	85.8	23.7	64	16.7	26.1

in that sample, and since it was the only sample which did not register a higher overall mean on the issue of exclusion of illegally seized evidence, it would seem that if the police felt that evidence should be excluded, it was because they thought it would be improper for the courts to admit it.

While the first two questions were general (what should happen when evidence has been illegally seized and a suspect is being tried), the third question focused on the consequences of the operation of the exclusionary rule: "A suspect who has been illegally searched gains too much by the exclusion of the illegally seized evidence" (*Suspect Gains Too Much*).

As can be seen from table 7-3, the police, recording an overall mean continuum score of 76.3, agreed strongly with this proposition. District attorneys, with a mean of 43.1, were somewhat of the opposite opinion, while defense attorneys, with a mean of 16.7, strongly believed that a suspect who has been illegally searched does not gain too much by the exclusion of the illegally seized evidence.

Thus, the police had been ambivalent about illegally seized evidence and its admissibility in court, but nonetheless felt quite strongly that the exclusion of illegally seized evidence does overcompensate the suspect. They objected not so much to the normative theoretical foundation of the exclusionary rule as to the consequences of its administration. If the ambit of the exclusionary rule were modified, their opposition might be lessened.[8] District attorneys, meanwhile, had shown themselves strong advocates of the normative rationale, but had been uncertain whether it overcompensates. Defense attorneys, finally, had been strong supporters of both the normative rationale and the idea that it is not an overcompensatory mechanism. As might be expected, the more strongly a respondent supported the normative rationale, the more strongly he felt that a suspect does not gain too much from the exclusionary rule.[9]

When responses were examined with regard to search and seizure perspectives, we noted that police officers with a low reasonable-low productive perspective were the most likely to feel that illegally searched suspects should have the evidence excluded in court, and the least likely to feel strongly that such action overcompensates the suspect. Conversely, officers with a high reasonable-high productive perspective were by far the most likely to feel that illegally searched suspects should not have the evidence excluded and the most likely to feel very strongly that such action overcompensates the suspect.[10] If these officers could be shown that there are in fact more searches which are unreasonable and unproductive than they perceive, then perhaps they would alter their attitude toward the exclusionary rule.

Overall, the findings show that there was good support for the normative rationale and hence the exclusionary rule in its present form. If, however, the exclusionary rule were modified so that suspects were not seen to be overcompensated, then this support might be far greater.

Conclusion

In this chapter an examination was undertaken of three possible positive functions performed by the exclusionary rule. Retaining the rule on the basis of the factual rationale (that is was performing positive deterrent or disciplinary functions) was found unwarranted. Not only did the exclusionary rule not deter in most circumstances, but when it did, it did so in a negative manner, and on the basis of limited knowledge of the law. In deciding whether to search, a police officer was likely to follow his own subjective assessment of the situation, which might or might not coincide with the court ruling. Moreover, none of the samples saw the exclusionary rule as fulfilling a disciplinary function, though all believed somewhat that a police officer does feel a personal loss when evidence he has seized is excluded in court.

Retention of the exclusionary rule was, however, supported on the strength of the normative rationale. Defense attorneys were strong advocates of the normative rationale and the idea that it is not an overcompensatory mechanism. While district attorneys were strong advocates of the normative rationale, they were uncertain whether it overcompensates suspects. The police were ambivalent about the merits of the normative rationale, and felt strongly that suspects are overcompensated, but their objections related not so much to the normative theoretical foundations of the rule as to the consequences of its administration. Thus, if the ambit of the rule were modified to lessen the extent to which it is presently seen as overcompensating, support for the rule on the basis of the normative rationale would be even greater.

Notes

1. 367 U.S. 643 (1961).

2. This third aspect may also work independently of the other two. For example, an individual may have moral inhibitions against an action which is at the same time legally proscribed. For a fuller discussion of deterrence, see, e.g., Johannes Andenaes, *Punishment and Deterrence* (Ann Arbor: University of Michigan Press, 1974); Franklin E. Zimring, *Perspectives on Deterrence* (Chevy Chase, Md: Center for Studies of Crime and Delinquency, National Institute of Mental Health, 1971); Franklin E. Zimring and Gordon J. Hawkins, *Deterrence: The Legal Threat in Crime Control* (Chicago: University of Chicago Press, 1973).

3. Correlations were .37 for police, .51 for district attorney, and .41 for defense attorney samples, respectively.

4. They were: (1) *General Discouraging Effect of Rule/Officer's Knowledge of Law:* .04** for the police, −.12** for district attorneys, and −.01** for defense attorneys; (2) *Officer's Knowledge of Law/Officer's Concern with Admissibility of Evidence:* .17*, .07**, and .01**, respectively.

5. $r = .55$

6. $r = .23*$

7. $r = -.03**$

8. Interestingly, the greater the number of suppression hearings an officer had been involved in during the previous year, the less inclined he was to believe that the introduction of such evidence would be improper ($r = -.43$ [$n = 87$]) and the more he tended to believe that the exclusion of such evidence overcompensates the suspect ($r = .20*$ [$n = 88$]).

9. The correlations were: (1) *Evidence Should be Excluded/Suspect Gains too much:* $-.45$ for police, $-.50$ for district attorneys, and $-.43$ for defense attorneys; (2) *Impropriety of Admitting Evidence/Suspect Gains too much:* $-.34$, $-.42$, and $-.43$ in the three samples, respectively.

10. The relevant figures were:

Reasonable Score	Productive Score	n	Evidence Should be Excluded		Suspect Gains Too Much	
			$\bar{x}$	s	$\bar{x}$	s
Low	Low	17	61.9	31.8	59.8	33.5
Low	High	12	52.8	32.3	78.7	24.7
Medium	Medium	24	52.5	37.2	79.8	27.6
High	Low	18	51.3	35.0	74.6	30.2
High	High	20	35.6	34.5	85.0	29.5

8 Proposed Modifications of the Exclusionary Rule

Introduction

The chapters up to now have examined feelings and perceptions of the present law of search and seizure. A general climate for change has been seen to exist, with the direction of the required move being toward the interests of law enforcement. Chapter seven indicated a lack of support for the exclusionary rule on the basis of the factual rationale, but a feeling for its retention in some form on the basis of the normative rationale. In this chapter an examination is undertaken of reactions to the proposed abolition of the rule, and to its limitation to cover only willful and excessive violations of Fourth Amendment rights.

Abolition

The most radical modification of the exclusionary rule that has been proposed is its abolition. Defense attorneys, with their civil libertarian interests and strong support for the normative rationale, might be expected to violently oppose abolition. In view of their strong support of the normative rationale, district attorneys might also be considered against the rule's abolition. The police might initially be expected to strongly favor abolition. However, when their ambivalent feelings about the normative rationale are considered (coupled with the general tendency of respondents to favor the status quo), this support might be hypothesized as less strong.

In order to evaluate support for abolition of the rule, respondents were asked to record their agreement or disagreement with the propositions that: "The Exclusionary Rule should be abolished" (*Abolition of Rule*) and "Reliable physical evidence should be admitted in criminal prosecutions regardless of the methods used in obtaining it" (*Admission of All Evidence*).

While the former question involved a direct choice, the latter suggested the desirability of the major direct effect of abolition. Though complementary, these questions are not identical. Thus, an individual might favor abolition of the rule, but at the same time feel that not all reliable physical evidence should be admitted regardless of the methods used in obtaining it. Alternatively, he might favor the introduction of all reliable physical evidence, but feel that other factors, such as the courts' regular overseeing of police conduct, militate against abolition.

Table 8-1 shows that the police, with a mean continuum score of 50.3, were undecided about exclusionary rule abolition. District attorneys, on the other hand, recording a mean score of 29.9, were strongly against abolition, while defense attorneys, with an overall mean of 8.9, were violently opposed.

Similar scores were obtained when we examined whether all reliable physical evidence should be admitted. The overall police mean was 52.8, the district attorney mean was 20.2, and the mean for defense attorneys was 9.4. The correlation between the two questions was .55 for police, .72 for district attorneys, and .81 for defense attorneys.

It is interesting that police officers in City A were somewhat opposed to the abolition propositions, while those in City B favored both to a slight extent.

Thus, while defense and prosecution officials were strongly opposed to abolition and the introduction of all reliable physical evidence, the police were ambivalent, with half for and half against the proposals. An examination of their responses in terms of background variables and search and seizure perspectives revealed some interesting trends. Officers who had worked on a gambling squad, or whose work function had been described as primarily investigation, were more favorably disposed to abolition and the introduction of all reliable physical evidence,[1] as were officers who had been involved in a greater number of suppression hearings or made a greater number of arrests during the previous year.[2] Similarly inclined were officers with high reasonable-high productive and high reasonable-low productive search and seizure perspectives. Thus, active participation in the occupation, and a perspective that police searches were for the most part reasonable, led to a heightened desire for the rule's abolition.

Chapter seven revealed strong support for the exclusionary rule on the basis of the normative rationale. To evaluate the strength of this rationale as an argument for the maintenance of the exclusionary rule, respondent answers were

Table 8-1
Abolition of the Exclusionary Rule

	Abolition of Rule			Admission of All evidence		
	n	$\bar{x}$	s	n	$\bar{x}$	s
Police						
City A	25	43.3	30.7	26	39.5	32.0
City B	68	52.9	31.7	68	57.9	33.1
All	93	50.3	31.6	94	52.8	33.7
District Attorneys						
Cities A and C	15	33.0	34.7	15	19.5	27.2
City B	30	28.3	30.4	30	20.6	25.0
All	45	29.9	31.6	45	20.2	25.4
Defense Attorneys						
Cities A and C	23	8.7	20.9	23	11.0	20.8
City B	41	9.0	12.8	41	8.5	12.9
All	64	8.9	16.0	64	9.4	16.1

correlated with those on abolition. The correlations between *Impropriety of Admitting Evidence/Abolition of Rule*, and *Impropriety of Admitting Evidence/Admission of All Evidence* were −.59 and −.46 for police, −.42 and −.70 for district attorneys, and −.73 and −.66 for defense attorneys. Similar high negative correlations were also found between *Evidence Should be Excluded* and both *Abolition of Rule* and *Admission of All Evidence*.[3] These high negative correlations attest to the significance of the normative rationale as an argument against the rule's abolition.

Two major effects that may be envisaged as a result of abolition of the exclusionary rule are increases in successful narcotics, gambling and weapons prosecutions, and in unreasonable police searches and seizures. To obtain perceptions of the likelihood of these outcomes, respondents were asked to scale their agreement or disagreement with the propostions: "If the exclusionary rule were abolished, the percentage of successful narcotics, gambling and weapons prosecutions would increase in the long run" (*Rule Abolished, Prosecutions Increase*), and "If the exclusionary rule were abolished, the percentage of 'unreasonable police searches and seizures' would increase in the long run" (*Rule Abolished, Unreasonable Searches Increase*). To measure whether respondents were willing to allow for an increase in de facto unreasonable searches and seizures in order to obtain a more successful rate of prosecutions, they were further asked to record their agreement or disagreement with the proposition: "An increase in the percentage of 'unreasonable police searches and seizures' would not matter, if there were also an increase in the percentage of successful narcotics, gambling and weapons prosecutions" (*Increase Unreasonable Searches OK if Successful Prosecutions Increase*).

From table 8-2 it can be seen that all three samples felt rather strongly that

Table 8-2
Effects of Abolition

	Rule Abolished, Successful Prosecutions Increase			Rule Abolished, Unreasonable Searches Increase			Increase Unreasonable Searches OK If Successful Prosecutions Increase		
	n	$\overline{x}$	s	n	$\overline{x}$	s	n	$\overline{x}$	s
Police									
City A	26	67.9	32.1	25	53.7	32.4	25	43.0	27.7
City B	68	82.2	23.7	65	58.0	28.2	68	43.7	28.6
All	94	78.3	26.9	90	56.8	29.3	93	43.5	28.2
District Attorneys									
Cities A and C	15	76.8	21.3	15	80.3	18.6	15	13.3	16.2
City B	29	82.0	19.9	30	74.9	22.4	29	16.8	16.4
All	44	80.2	20.3	45	76.7	21.1	44	15.6	16.2
Defense Attorneys									
Cities A and C	23	78.9	24.6	23	89.8	12.4	23	5.9	7.3
City B	41	76.6	30.4	41	85.6	22.6	38	8.8	14.2
All	64	77.4	28.2	64	87.1	19.6	61	7.7	12.0

abolition of the exclusionary rule would result in a greater success rate for narcotics, gambling, and weapons prosecutions; the overall police mean score was 78.3, the district attorney mean was 80.2, and the defense attorney mean was 77.4. The police, recording a mean score of 56.8, thought only to a slight extent that abolition of the exclusionary rule would result in a greater percentage of unreasonable police searches and seizures. Prosecution officials, with a mean of 76.7, and defense officials, with a mean of 87.1 were, however, strongly inclined to believe that the rate of unreasonable searches and seizures would increase. Interestingly enough, while the police believed far more strongly that successful prosecutions would increase than that unreasonable searches would, and district attorneys were slightly inclined to that same view, defense attorneys were stronger in believing that unreasonable searches and seizures would increase. Only in the district attorney sample was there any significant correlation between these two questions.[4]

The police, with a mean continuum score of 43.5, were very slightly negative about the proposition that an increase in unreasonable police searches and seizures would not matter if there were also an increase in successful narcotics, gambling, and weapons prosecutions. Prosecution officials, with a mean of 15.6, and defense officials, with a mean of 7.7, were very negative about that proposition. The more a defense attorney believed that unreasonable police searches would increase if the exclusionary rule were abolished, the more strongly he felt that such an increase would not be compensated by an increase in successful prosecutions.[5] Conversely, the more strongly a police officer felt that successful prosecutions would increase if the exclusionary rule were abolished, the more inclined he was to believe that an increase in unreasonable searches and seizures did not matter.[6]

In chapter seven we found that the police were somewhat inclined to consider the exclusionary rule a deterrent, but neither district attorneys nor defense officials were inclined to share this belief. When these responses were correlated with projections of whether unreasonable searches and seizures would increase if the exclusionary rule were abolished, it was found that only in the police sample was there even a slightly significant correlation between the two.[7] Thus, those who believed the rule deterred seemed to feel that those who were deterred would be deterred from making illegal searches anyway, whether or not the rule existed. Conversely, those who did not consider the rule a deterrent, but thought that unreasonable searches and seizures would increase if the rule were abolished, seem to be voicing the fear that abandonment of the rule would actually encourage police to make more unreasonable searches and seizures.

There was virtually no support for abolition of the exclusionary rule; much of the opposition to abolition stemmed from the normative rationale. Although there was strong belief that successful narcotics, gambling, and weapons prosecutions would increase, also voiced was a general fear that unlawful searches and seizures would rise. Overall, respondents felt that an increase in successful prosecutions would not compensate for the increase in unlawful searches, and a sentiment was discerned suggesting that abolition of the rule might actually encourage police to engage in a larger number of unreasonable searches and seizures.

Limitation to Willful and Excessive Violations

Both the American Law Institute proposal[8] and Senator Bentsen's congressional bill[9] would limit the exclusionary rule to situations where the violation of Fourth Amendment rights was found to be "substantial." As expected, early pretesting indicated considerable difficulty with the term "substantial." By substituting the phrase "willful and excessive" (suggested by responses to the open-ended question "What sort of violations do you consider to be 'substantial?' ") we hoped both to preserve the essence of the proposed modification[10] and to present respondents with a less nebulous term with a more generally acceptable core of application.

Since modification of the exclusionary rule to cover only willful and excessive violations is a compromise between the interests of law enforcement and civil liberties that safeguards to some degree the normative rationale, the defense attorney opposition to this proposal might be less forceful than it was to the rule's abolition. In turn, the district attorneys, with their ambivalence over the exclusionary rule's possible overcompensation of suspects, might be more in favor of such a compromise. Finally, the police might again be expected to split, with some for, and some against such a proposal.

To estimate the percentage of unreasonable searches that might be affected by this modification of the exclusionary rule, police officers and prosecution and defense officials were asked: "In your opinion, what percentage of all violations of the Fourth Amendment's prohibition against unreasonable search and seizure is 'willful and excessive' "? (*Percentage Violations Willful and Excessive*). A ten-centimeter line, whose ends were labeled *0%* and *100%* respectively, was provided for recording responses.

From table 8-3 it can be seen that the police, with a mean continuum score of 27.0%, and the district attorneys, with 27.5%, considered a far lower percentage of violations of the Fourth Amendment as willful and excessive than did defense attorneys, who recorded a mean of 55.6%. Interestingly, the more arrests a police officer had made during the previous year, the fewer violations of the Fourth Amendment he thought were willful and excessive.[11]

To gauge the receptivity of respondents to a limitation of the exclusionary rule to cover only willful and excessive violations, respondents were asked for scaled agreement or disagreement with the proposition that: "Reliable physical evidence should be admitted in criminal prosecutions unless the violation of the suspect's Fourth Amendment rights was 'willful and excessive' " (*Evidence Admitted Unless Violation Willful and Excessive*).

Table 8-3
Limitation of the Exclusionary Rule to Willful and Excessive Violations

	Percentage Violations Willful and Excessive			Evidence Admitted Unless Violation Willful and Excessive			Rule Limited, Unreasonable Searches Increase		
	n	$\overline{x}$	s	n	$\overline{x}$	s	n	$\overline{x}$	s
Police									
City A	25	33.2	26.9	26	57.8	39.0	26	44.0	32.3
City B	67	24.7	18.2	68	65.7	31.0	68	52.5	28.3
All	92	27.0	21.1	94	63.4	33.4	94	50.1	29.5
District Attorneys									
Cities A and C	15	24.8	23.5	15	41.9	35.6	15	71.7	27.0
City B	29	28.9	26.2	30	41.1	35.4	30	56.9	29.7
All	44	27.5	25.1	45	41.4	35.0	45	61.8	29.4
Defense Attorneys									
Cities A and C	23	59.7	26.8	23	15.1	23.2	23	76.8	31.2
City B	40	53.2	26.1	41	13.8	23.0	41	62.9	36.2
All	63	55.6	26.3	64	14.3	22.9	64	67.9	34.9

Table 8-3 reveals that the police, with a mean continuum score of 63.4, were somewhat in favor of such a modification, while the district attorneys, with 41.4, were somewhat against it, and the defense attorneys, with 14.3, were strongly opposed. The greater the number of arrests a police officer had made, the more likely he was to favor the limitation,[12] while the greater the number of years a district attorney had worked in the district attorney's office the more inclined he was to take such an attitude.[13]

Thus the police registered greater support for this proposal than they had for the rule's abolition; district attorneys and even defense attorneys were less vehement in their opposition. Indeed, police support was slightly stronger when allowance was made for those who had supported the rule's abolition but were against limiting it to willful and excessive violations.[14] Overall, those who supported a limitation of the exclusionary rule to cover only willful and excessive violations had also tended to support abolition.[15]

When we examined the extent to which views on modification were influenced by perceptions of how many searches would be affected by the modification, we found that respondents who considered a greater percentage of unreasonable searches and seizures willful and excessive tended to be less favorably inclined to limit the ambit of the exclusionary rule to such searches.[16] Perhaps those who saw a larger percentage of unreasonable searches and seizures as willful and excessive were voicing a lack of confidence in the police; hence their unwillingness to alter the rule.

A major source of opposition to the rule's abolition stemmed, as it may be recalled, from support of the normative rationale. To evaluate the strength of this rationale as an argument against modifying the exclusionary rule, respondent answers to *Evidence Admitted unless Violation Willful and Excessive* were correlated with *Impropriety of Admitting Evidence* and *Evidence should be*

Excluded. The ensuing correlations were −.12** and −.20* for police, −.37 and −.56 for prosecution, and −.30 and −.17** for defense attorneys. While these correlations suggest that the normative rationale was a factor in the opposition to exclusionary rule modification, its significance was nowhere as great as it had been in the case of abolition. Thus, modification of the rule to cover willful and excessive violations appears to be a compromise between the interests of law enforcement and of civil liberties, which would to some extent satisfy the needs of proponents of the normative rationale.

To obtain respondent evaluations of the potential effect of this proposed modification, we asked them to scale their agreement or disagreement with the statement: "If illegally seized evidence were excluded only when the search was 'willful and excessive,' the percentage of 'unreasonable police searches and seizures' would increase" (*Rule Limited, Unreasonable Searches Increase*).

As can be seen from table 8-3, police, with an overall mean continuum score of 50.1, were ambivalent about this proposition, while prosecution and defense officials, with means of 61.8 and 67.9, respectively, felt to some extent that "unreasonable police searches and seizures" would increase if illegally seized evidence were excluded only when the search was "willful and excessive."

Only in the defense attorney sample was any background variable found to account for significant variation in response. Defense attorneys who had handled a greater number of suppression hearings during the previous year were less likely to believe that unreasonable police searches and seizures would increase.[17]

When these responses are compared with those concerning whether unreasonable searches and seizures would increase if the rule were abolished, all samples felt less strongly that modification would increase them. Those who felt there would be an increase if the rule were abolished also tended to believe there would be an increase if the rule were modified to cover willful and excessive violations.[18] Only district attorneys appeared to oppose modifying the exclusionary rule because of a fear that unreasonable searches and seizures would increase.[19] As with abolition, there was almost no correlation between views on the deterrent effect of the rule and those on the likelihood that unreasonable searches would increase if the rule were limited to willful and excessive violations.[20] This again suggested a concern that the police should not, as a result of the rule's modification, feel encouraged to do virtually as they wish.

Overall, then, there was greater support for limitation of the exclusionary rule to cover willful and excessive violations than there had been for its abolition, with less fear of an increase in unreasonable searches and seizures, and less opposition on the basis of the normative rationale.

Conclusion

In this chapter we examined the receptivity of respondents to two proposed modifications of the exclusionary rule, and their perceptions of the likely effects of the changes.

Abolition of the rule received virtually no support, with much of the opposition stemming from the normative rationale. While there was strong feeling that successful prosecutions would increase, there was also concern that there would be more unreasonable searches and seizures if the rule were abolished. Overall, it was felt that an increase in successful prosecutions would not compensate for the increase in unlawful searches and seizures, and a sentiment was discerned suggesting that abolition of the rule might actually encourage the police to engage in a greater number of unreasonable searches and seizures.

Limitation of the rule to cover willful and excessive violations of Fourth Amendment rights received greater support, with less opposition on the basis of the normative rationale and less fear that an increase in unreasonable searches and seizures would occur. Some opposition appeared to be the result of lack of confidence in the police, and a trend was observed which again suggested that measures be taken to ensure that the police do not feel, as a result of the rule's modification, that they enjoy greater license to search at will.

Notes

1. The relevant correlations were: worked on gambling squad/abolition of rule: $r = .47$; worked on gambling squad/admission of all evidence: $r = .33$. The means for work function were:

Work Description	Abolition of Rule			Admission of All Evidence		
	n	$\bar{x}$	s	n	$\bar{x}$	s
Patrol	46	46.5	32.0	46	48.7	34.4
Investigation	23	61.2	30.1	23	65.2	30.4
Supervision and/or administration	14	48.4	32.1	15	51.0	36.9

2. The relevant correlations were:

	Abolition of Rule	Admission of All Evidence
Number of suppression hearings involved in during the last year	.30	.38
Number of arrests made during the last year	.18* (n=89)	.19* (n=89)

3. The correlations were:

	Evidence Should Be Excluded/Abolition of Rule	Evidence Should Be Excluded/Admission of All Evidence
Police	−.52	−.41
District attorneys	−.71	−.70
Defense attorneys	−.60	−.66

4. $r = .33*$.

5. $r = −.77$.

6. $r = .23*$.

7. The relevant correlations were: (1) *General Discouraging Effect of Rule/Rule Abolished, Unreasonable Searches Increase:* .20* for police, −.20** for district attorneys, .19** for defense attorneys; (2) *Officer's Concern with Admissibility of Evidence/Rule Abolished, Unreasonable Searches Increase:* −.06**, .15** and .02** in the three samples, respectively.

8. American Law Institute, *A Model Code of Pre-Arraignment Procedure: Proposed Official Draft* (Philadelphia: The American Law Institute, 1975) Sec. SS 290.2 (2).

9. U.S. Congress, Senate, *A bill to amend title 18 of the United States Code to define and limit the exclusionary rule in federal criminal proceedings,* Ninety-third Congress, First Session, 1973, S. 881.

10. Analytically it may be seen that this phrase does preserve the essence of the proposed modification. The ALI proposal states that in determining whether a violation is substantial

. . . the court shall consider all the circumstances including:
(a) the extent of deviation from lawful conduct;
(b) the extent to which the violation was willful;
(c) the extent to which privacy was invaded;
(d) the extent to which exclusion will tend to prevent violations of this code;
(e) whether, but for the violation, the things seized would have been discovered; and
(f) the extent to which the violation prejudiced the moving party's ability to support his motion, or to defend himself in the proceedings in which the things seized are sought to be offered in evidence against him.

American Law Institute, *Model Code* Sec. SS 290.2 (4). Senator Bentsen's bill contains the same provisions with a few very minor changes in wording; U.S. Congress, Senate, *Bill to amend title 18,* S. 881.

11. $r = .37$.

12. $r = .24*$.

13. $r = .28*$.

14. When we omitted respondents scoring more than 60 on *Admission of all Evidence* but less than 60 on *Evidence Admitted unless Violation Willful and Excessive*, the mean score on the latter variable rose to 70.4 ($n = 80$, $s = 30.1$). Respondents who were omitted had at least a forty-point differential between scores on the two questions. When a similar run was made utilizing *Abolition of Rule* instead of *Admission of All Evidence*, the mean score on *Evidence Admitted unless Violation Willful and Excessive* became 68.0 ($n = 84$, $s = 31.6$). When these two computer runs were repeated in prosecution and defense samples, their mean scores on *Evidence Admitted unless Violation Willful and Excessive* rose very slightly.

15. The relevant correlations were: (1) *Evidence Admitted unless Violation Willful and Excessive/Abolition of Rule*: .24* for police, .46 for district attorneys, and .38 for defense attorneys; (2) *Evidence Admitted unless Violation Willful and Excessive/Admission of All Evidence*: .00**, .50, and .33 for the three samples, respectively.

16. The relevant correlations were: police, $r = -.28$; district attorneys, $r = -.29*$; and defense, $r = -.16**$.

17. $r = -.30$.

18. The correlations were: police, $r = .18*$; district attorneys, $r = .38$; defense attorneys, $r = .39$.

19. $r = -.28*$.

20. The relevant correlations were: (1) *General Discouraging Effect of Rule/Rule Limited, Unreasonable Searches Increase*: .17* for police, −.05** for district attorneys and .14** for defense attorneys; (2) *Officer's Concern with Admissibility of Evidence/Rule Limited, Unreasonable Searches Increase*: .10**, .09** and −.11** in the three samples, respectively.

9 The Issuance and Enforcement of Police Rules of Conduct

Introduction

A positive attribute of the exclusionary rule which would be lost if it were abolished, and diminished if it were limited to cover only willful and excessive violations, is the regular overseeing by the courts of police conduct relating to search and seizure. Though the courts are regularly involved in this type of function, the manner in which they issue and enforce their guidelines on search and seizure is unclear and indirect. In this chapter respondents were asked for their views on who should issue and who should enforce police rules of conduct regarding search and seizure. This allowed us to compare the present and the desired situation, and gave an indication of the mood for change.

The Issuance of Police Rules of Conduct

Though in theory there are a number of authorities who could issue police rules of conduct in the area of search and seizure, this is a task which for the most part has been left for the courts. In order to canvass respondent opinions we gave them a list of the possible choices:

The most suitable body for issuing police rules of conduct in the area of search and seizure is:
a. The legislature
b. The courts
c. A police authority
d. A police-civilian authority
e. A civilian authority
f. A combination of the above. Please explain _____.
g. Other. Please explain _____.

Table 9-1 reveals that twenty-nine police officers (30.9%) considered a police authority acting alone as the best body for issuing police rules of conduct, while eighteen (19.1%) favored the legislature, and the same number, the courts. Seven (7.4%) were for a police-civilian authority, and six (6.4%) for a combination of the courts and police. All in all, as table 9-2 shows, when combination votes were considered, forty-six officers (54.1%) chose the police, thirty (35.3%) the courts, and twenty-four (28.2%) the legislature. Only eight (9.4%) would give any authority to civilians.[1]

Table 9-1
Issuing Police Rules of Conduct: Authority Recommended

	Legis-lature	Courts	Police	Police-Civilian Body	Civilian	Legis-lature/ Courts	Legis-lature/ Police-Civilian Body	Courts/ Police	Courts/ Police-Civilian Body	Courts/ Civilian
Police										
City A	7 26.9%	7 26.9%	6 23.1%	1 3.8%	—	—	—	2 7.7%	—	—
City B	11 16.2%	11 16.2%	23 33.8%	6 8.8%	—	3 4.4%	1 1.5%	4 5.9%	—	—
All	18 19.1%	18 19.1%	29 30.9%	7 7.4%	—	3 3.2%	1 1.1%	6 6.4%	—	—
District Attorneys										
Cities A & C	1 7.1%	4 28.6%	2 14.3%	1 7.1%	—	—	—	2 14.3%	—	—
City B	4 13.8%	8 27.6%	3 10.3%	4 13.8%	—	3 10.3%	—	1 3.4%	—	—
All	5 11.6%	12 27.9%	5 11.6%	5 11.6%	—	3 7.0%	—	3 7.0%	—	—
Defense Attorneys										
Cities A & C	4 18.2%	6 27.6%	1 4.5%	2 9.1%	1 4.5%	4 18.2%	—	1 4.5%	1 4.5%	—
City B	3 7.7%	5 12.8%	4 10.3%	11 28.2%	2 5.1%	3 7.7%	—	—	1 2.6%	1 2.6%
All	7 11.5%	11 18.0%	5 8.2%	13 21.3%	3 4.9%	7 11.5%	—	1 1.6%	2 3.3%	1 1.6%

	Legislature/ Courts/ Police	Legislature/ Courts/ Police-Civilian Body	Courts/ Police/ Civilian	Courts/ and Some Police Voice	Police/ Civilian/ Bar Association	Police/ District Attorney	District Attorney	Legislature/ Courts/ Police/ Civilian	Courts/ Police/ District Attorney	Unexplained Combination
Police										
City A	1 / 3.8%	—	—	—	—	—	—	—	—	2 / 7.7%
City B	1 / 1.5%	—	—	1 / 1.5%	—	—	—	—	—	7 / 10.3%
All	2 / 2.1%	—	—	1 / 1.1%	—	—	—	—	—	9 / 9.6%
District Attorneys										
Cities A & C	—	1 / 7.1%	—	—	—	1 / 7.1%	1 / 7.1%	—	—	1 / 7.1%
City B	1 / 3.4%	—	1 / 3.4%	—	—	—	1 / 3.4%	1 / 3.4%	1 / 3.4%	1 / 3.4%
All	1 / 2.3%	1 / 2.3%	1 / 2.3%	—	—	1 / 2.3%	2 / 4.7%	1 / 2.3%	1 / 2.3%	2 / 4.7%
Defense Attorneys										
Cities A & C	—	—	—	—	2 / 5.1%	—	1 / 4.5%	—	—	1 / 4.5%
City B	1 / 2.6%	1 / 2.6%	—	—	—	—	—	1 / 2.6%	—	4 / 10.3%
All	1 / 1.6%	1 / 1.6%	—	—	2 / 3.3%	—	1 / 1.6%	1 / 1.6%	—	5 / 8.2%

Table 9-2
Issuing Police Rules of Conduct: Combination Votes

	Legisla-ture	Courts	Police	Civilian	Bar Asso-ciation	District Attorney
Police	24	30	46	8	–	–
	28.2%	35.3%	54.1%	9.4%		
District Attorneys	11	23	19	8	–	4
	26.8%	56.1%	46.3%	19.5%		9.8%
Defense Attorneys	17	25	26	23	2	1
	30.4%	44.6%	46.4%	41.1%	3.6%	1.8%

In the district attorney sample, twelve (27.9%) favored the courts and five each (11.6%) the legislature, the police and a police-civilian authority. In addition, four (9.8%) inserted a reply that included the district attorney's office.

In the defense attorney sample thirteen (21.3%) favored a police-civilian authority, eleven (18.0%) favored the courts, and seven each (11.5%) chose either the legislature or the legislature and the courts. Only five (8.2%) considered a police authority alone as the best body for issuing rules of conduct. When combined preferences were considered, however, we noted that twenty-six (46.4%) defense attorneys mentioned the police, twenty-five (44.6%) mentioned the courts, twenty-three (41.1%) cited a civilian authority, and seventeen (30.4%) the legislature. In addition, two (3.6%) defense attorneys added a reply that included the bar association, and one (1.8%) included the district attorney's office.

From these figures it can be seen that about half of each sample felt that the police should have some say in the issuance of police rules of conduct. An equally large percentage (though appreciably lower in the police sample and slightly higher in that of the district attorneys) thought that the courts should be involved, while about a quarter of each sample saw legislative participation as desirable. Over two-fifths of the defense attorneys considered that civilians should be involved in the issuance of such rules, but under one-fifth of the district attorneys and less than one-tenth of the police thought civilian participation desirable.

To test the effect of knowledge of the existence of civilian review boards upon response, those sampled were asked: "Do you know of either a police-civilian or a civilian authority being used at any time in [your state] to review police action?"

The answers were revealing. While twenty-nine (30.9%) of police respondents claimed they were aware of such an authority being used, none of the eight who favored civilian participation in the issuance of police rules of conduct did. Similar but far less striking trends were observed in the prosecution and defense samples.

Observation of variation in response with regard to background variables showed that police officers who had been frequently involved in suppression hearings during the previous year were less likely to favor the courts and more likely to select a police authority.[2] This indicates a greater lack of confidence in the courts and, perhaps, a desire to avoid the judicial process on the part of those officers most experienced with suppression hearings.

About half of each sample felt that the police should have some say in the issuance of police rules of conduct. When this issue was taken one step further, and respondents were asked whether: "Police departments should issue detailed regulations describing when and how police officers should undertake searches" (*Issuance of Detailed Regulations by Police Departments*), all samples felt strongly that police departments should issue detailed regulations on search and seizure. While the police registered an overall mean score of 66.9, district attorneys recorded 76.6, and defense attorneys 83.8. (See table 9-3.) Police officers who had made a greater number of arrests during the previous year, or who had worked on a tactical task force, favored less strongly the issuance of detailed regulations,[3] while those who described their primary work as supervision and/or administration were more inclined to favor it.[4]

In terms of issuing police rules of conduct relating to search and seizure, then, there was a general demand for police involvement. The courts received reasonable support for the role they have been playing in this task, but respondents indicated the need for input from other quarters. In addition to the police, a fair percentage of respondents considered that the legislature ought to participate. Only defense attorneys showed much support for the idea of civilian involvement.

The Enforcement of Police Rules of Conduct

A number of authorities could be responsible for overseeing the enforcement of police rules of conduct. This too is a function which has been largely left to the

Table 9-3
Issuance of Detailed Regulations by Police Departments

	n	$\bar{x}$	s
Police			
City A	26	72.4	32.4
City B	66	64.8	34.4
All	92	66.9	33.8
District Attorneys			
Cities A and C	15	91.1	18.9
City B	29	69.6	31.5
All	44	76.6	29.5
Defense Attorneys			
Cities A and C	23	80.7	26.0
City B	41	85.7	19.0
All	64	83.8	21.7

courts. To obtain respondent opinions on who should be entrusted with this
responsibility, we presented them with a list of choices:

> The most suitable body for overseeing the enforcement of police rules
> of conduct in the area of search and seizure is:
> a.   The courts
> b.   A police authority
> c.   A police-civilian authority
> d.   A civilian authority
> e.   A combination of the above. Please explain _____.
> f.   Other. Please explain _____.

Respondents tended to select the same body they had chosen for issuing
rules of conduct. Here, however, the legislature was not one of the response
categories presented. Despite this, fifty-five (78.8%) of the seventy police
officers who could make the same choice did so, as did fifteen (45.%) of the
thirty-three district attorneys and twenty-three (52.3%) of the forty-four
defense attorneys. Where there was a change in selection, the move was generally
toward the courts.

An examination of the responses shows (see table 9-4) that thirty-seven
(39.4%) of the police officers chose a police authority, thirty-two (34.0%) the
courts, and ten (10.6%) a police-civilian authority. Six (6.4%) favored a
combination of courts and police. When all explained combinations were taken
into consideration, a total of fifty-five respondents (63.2%) mentioned the
police, forty (46.0%) the courts, and eleven (12.6%), civilians. (See table 9-5.)

In the district attorney sample, eighteen (41.9%) selected the courts, and
eight (18.6%) each a police or police-civilian authority. Three (7.0%) chose a
combination of the courts and police. When combination selections were
examined, we found that twenty-two (56.4%) district attorneys mentioned
court, twenty-one (53.8%) police, and nine (23.1%) civilian participation. In
addition, one district attorney (2.6%) mentioned the bar association and one the
district attorney's office.

In the defense attorney sample, twenty-eight (45.9%) selected the courts
alone, fourteen (23.0%) a police-civilian authority, and five (8.2%) a combination of the courts and a police-civilian authority. When combination votes
were considered, it was noted that thirty-eight (65.5%) defense attorneys
mentioned the courts, twenty-six (44.8%) mentioned a civilian authority, and
twenty-five (43.1%) a police authority. One (1.7%) defense attorney included
the district attorney's office.

Respondents who opted for civilian participation were less likely to know of
either a police-civilian or civilian authority being used at any time in their state
to review police action. Again, this was most striking in the police sample, where
none of the eleven officers who favored civilian involvement knew of such an
authority.

Table 9-4
Overseeing the Enforcement of Police Rules of Conduct: Authority Recommended

	Courts	Police	Police-Civilian Body	Civilian	Courts/Police	Courts/Police-Civilian Body	Courts/Civilian	Courts/Police/Police-Civilian Body	Courts and some Police Voice	Police/District Attorney	Police-Civilian Body/D.A.	Courts/Police-Civilian Body/Civilian/Bar Association	Unexplained Combination
Police													
City A	9 34.6%	9 34.6%	1 3.8%	—	4 15.4%	—	—	—	—	—	—	—	3 11.5%
City B	23 33.8%	28 41.2%	9 13.2%	—	2 2.9%	1 1.5%	—	—	1 1.5%	—	—	—	4 5.9%
All	32 34.0%	37 39.4%	10 10.6%	—	6 6.4%	1 1.1%	—	—	1 1.1%	—	—	—	7 7.4%
District Attorneys													
Cities A & C	5 35.7%	5 35.7%	1 7.1%	—	—	—	—	—	—	1 7.1%	—	—	2 14.3%
City B	13 44.8%	3 10.3%	7 24.1%	—	3 10.3%	—	—	—	—	—	—	1 3.4%	2 6.9%
All	18 41.9%	8 18.6%	8 18.6%	—	3 7.0%	—	—	—	—	1 2.3%	—	1 2.3%	4 9.3%
Defense Attorneys													
Cities A & C	12 52.2%	1 4.3%	4 17.4%	—	—	4 17.4%	1 4.3%	—	—	—	1 4.3%	—	—
City B	16 42.1%	1 2.6%	10 26.3%	3 7.9%	2 5.3%	1 2.6%	1 2.6%	1 2.6%	—	—	—	—	3 7.9%
All	28 45.9%	2 3.3%	14 23.0%	3 4.9%	2 3.3%	5 8.2%	2 3.3%	1 1.6%	—	—	1 1.6%	—	3 4.9%

Table 9-5
Overseeing the Enforcement of Police Rules of Conduct: Combination Votes

	Courts	Police	Civilian	Bar Association	District Attorney
Police	40	55	11	–	–
	46.0%	63.2%	12.6%		
District Attorneys	22	21	9	1	1
	56.4%	53.8%	23.1%	2.6%	2.6%
Defense Attorneys	38	25	26	–	1
	65.5%	43.1%	44.8%		1.7%

When background variables were examined as a source of variation in response, it was noted that police officers who had made more arrests or been involved in more suppression hearings during the previous year were less likely to favor the courts and more likely to select the police.[5]

Conclusion

Overall, then, when respondents were asked who should have the responsibility for functions presently left to the courts, there was only fair support for the courts, indicating the necessity for change in this area. There was more support for court enforcement of rules than court issuance of the rules. While legislative involvement in the issuance of rules was advocated by a substantial minority, all samples showed strong support for police involvement in both roles. The police, naturally, favored the strongest police participation, while district attorneys, and especially defense attorneys, favored a more diluted police role. Conversely, defense attorneys were the greatest advocates of civilian participation, while the police were the least enthusiastic.

Notes

1. Unexplained combinations were omitted from the percentage calculations.
2. Out of the seventy-two police officers who had been involved in ten or fewer suppression hearings, seventeen (23.6%) chose the courts and nineteen (26.4%) the police. Out of the seventeen officers who had been involved in more than ten suppression hearings, one (5.9%) chose the courts and eight (47.1%) chose the police. A similar, but less striking trend was observed with regard to the number of warrantless felony and misdemeanor arrests an officer had made during the previous year.
3. The correlations were: (1) *Number of warrantless misdemeanor and*

felony arrests made during the past year and *Issuance of Detailed Regulations by Police Departments:* $-.21^*$ (n = 87); (2) *Worked on tactical task force* and *Issuance of Detailed Regulations by Police Departments:* $-.34$ (n = 70).

4. The relevant figures were:

Work Description	Issuance of Detailed Regulations by Police Departments		
	n	$\bar{x}$	s
Patrol	46	63.8	35.5
Investigation	22	64.5	36.1
Supervision/administration	15	84.2	21.2

5. Out of the thirty-two officers who had made ten or fewer warrantless felony and misdemeanor arrests the previous year, fifteen (46.9%) selected the courts, and seven (21.9%) selected the police. Out of the fifty-seven officers who had made more than ten such arrests, seventeen (29.8%) chose the courts, and twenty-seven (47.4%) the police. While twenty-nine (40.3%) of the officers involved in ten or fewer suppression hearings chose the courts, and twenty-six (36.1%) the police, only three (17.6%) out of the seventeen involved in more than ten hearings selected the courts, and eight (47.1%) the police.

10 Receptivity to Alternatives to the Exclusionary Rule

Introduction

In previous chapters we examined perceptions of the various functions performed by the exclusionary rule, and of views on proposals to abolish or modify it. We also attempted to determine which body was considered the best for issuing, and which for enforcing police rules of conduct in search and seizure. In this chapter we will study the receptivity of respondents to alternatives to the exclusionary rule, and the opinions about when such alternatives should be applied.

The problem of ensuring compliance with the Fourth Amendment was stated in chapter one to be twofold. First, there is the question of how to protect the public by deterring government officials from making unreasonable searches and seizures. And second, when such protection has been insufficient, there is the question of how to punish the errant official and compensate the wronged individual. Chapter two discussed the infrequent use of civil, criminal, and administrative actions, and their consequent ineffectiveness as deterrents. This chapter describes respondent views on the use of these actions. Disciplinary and compensatory mechanisms were presented to respondents, who indicated how such mechanisms might fit in a framework that would better ensure the Fourth Amendment's guarantee against unreasonable search and seizure. Since the exclusionary rule can only operate when contraband or incriminating evidence is found, an important matter for investigation was whether these other actions should be more readily available when an unreasonable search and seizure has not uncovered contraband or incriminating evidence.

Compensation

Compensation may be described here as the monetary redress a wronged individual receives for the violation of his Fourth Amendment rights. It is also a mechanism which may discourage future violations by imposing a financial liability upon the offending officer or the governmental unit which employs him. The focus is on the injuries suffered, and redress is generally through an action in the courts.

To find out what types of injury respondents thought should be compensated, they were asked:

Regardless of the availability of other procedures, a person whose
Fourth Amendment rights have been violated should receive monetary
compensation when he has suffered (Please mark all that apply):
a.   Personal injury
b.   Severe mental anguish
c.   Loss of property
d.   Loss of wages
e.   None of the above
f.   Other. Please explain _____.

Table 10-1 shows that there was considerable support for the idea that a
person whose Fourth Amendment rights have been violated should receive
monetary compensation when he has suffered personal injury. This opinion was,
indeed, voiced by 66.0% of the police, 76.2% of the district attorneys, and
91.9% of the defense attorneys. In addition, 38.3% of the police, 73.8% of the
district attorneys, and 85.5% of the defense attorneys felt that compensation for
loss of property should be paid, while 42.6%, 57.1%, and 80.6% respectively
favored compensation for loss of wages. Finally, 22.3% of the police, 35.7% of
the prosecution, and 64.5% of the defense sample felt that an injured party
should be compensated for severe mental anguish.

The defense attorney sample consistently had the largest percentage favoring compensation, and the police sample the smallest. While the police as a
whole recommended compensation only for personal injury, district attorneys
also favored payment for loss of property and wages, but not for severe mental
anguish. Only defense attorneys as a whole approved of compensation in all four
cases. In all three samples, the strongest support was for compensation for
personal injury, and the weakest for compensation for severe mental anguish.
While more prosecution and defense officials supported compensation for loss of
property than for loss of wages, the opposite was true for police officers.

The most commonly proposed additional category of compensation was for
character defamation or loss of dignity, which was suggested by one police
officer, one district attorney, and four defense attorneys. Four other defense
attorneys favored punitive or exemplary damages, while another four recommended that the illegally searched person receive a variation of out-of-pocket
expenses and compensation for inconvenience or attorney fees. Five write-in
responses proposed that compensation be paid "only if the victim were
innocent," and three specified "only if the violation were intentional, gross or
excessive." Three favored compensation "in all cases," and three "never."

Composite scores were determined by totalling affirmative answers for each
major type of compensation. Police averaged 1.7 affirmative responses, district
attorneys 2.4, and defense attorneys 3.2. (See table 10-2.)

When the composite scores were examined with regard to background
variables, it was noted that district attorneys who were younger, or who had
spent fewer years in law practice, were more likely to answer affirmatively to a

Table 10-1
Payment of Compensation

	Personal Injury		Severe Mental Anguish		Loss of Property		Loss of Wages		None of the above		Other
	Yes	No	Yes	No	Yes	No	Yes	No	Yes	No	
Police											
City A	15 57.7%	11 42.3%	7 26.9%	19 73.1%	10 38.5%	16 61.5%	12 46.2%	14 53.8%	8 30.8%	18 69.2%	2
City B	47 69.1%	21 30.9%	14 20.6%	54 79.4%	26 38.2%	42 61.8%	28 41.2%	40 58.8%	13 19.4%	54 80.6%	4
All	62 66.0%	32 34.0%	21 22.3%	73 77.7%	36 38.3%	58 61.7%	40 42.6%	54 57.4%	21 22.6%	72 77.4%	6
District Attorneys											
Cities A & C	12 80.0%	3 20.0%	3 20.0%	12 80.0%	12 80.0%	3 20.0%	10 66.7%	5 33.3%	2 13.3%	13 86.7%	1
City B	20 74.1%	7 25.9%	12 44.4%	15 55.6%	19 70.4%	8 29.6%	14 51.9%	13 48.1%	6 23.1%	20 76.9%	4
All	32 76.2%	10 23.8%	15 35.7%	27 64.3%	31 73.8%	11 26.2%	24 57.1%	18 42.9%	8 19.5%	33 80.5%	5
Defense Attorneys											
Cities A & C	22 95.7%	1 4.3%	13 56.5%	10 43.5%	19 82.6%	4 17.4%	19 82.6%	4 17.4%	1 4.3%	22 95.7%	7
City B	35 89.7%	4 10.3%	27 69.2%	12 30.8%	34 87.2%	5 12.8%	31 79.5%	8 20.5%	3 8.3%	33 91.7%	10
All	57 91.9%	5 8.1%	40 64.5%	22 35.5%	53 85.5%	9 14.5%	50 80.6%	12 19.4%	4 6.8%	55 93.2%	17

Compensation should be paid for

Table 10-2

Number of Compensation Categories to Which an Affirmative Answer Was Given

	0	1	2	3	4	n	$\bar{x}$	s
Police								
City A	8	5	4	5	4	26	1.7	1.5
	30.8%	19.2%	15.4%	19.2%	15.4%			
City B	13	26	9	9	11	68	1.7	1.4
	19.1%	38.2%	13.2%	13.2%	16.2%			
All	21	31	13	14	15	94	1.7	1.4
	22.3%	33.0%	13.8%	14.9%	16.0%			
District Attorneys								
Cities A & C	2	1	3	6	3	15	2.5	1.3
	13.3%	6.7%	20.0%	40.0%	20.0%			
City B	6	2	4	5	10	27	2.4	1.6
	22.2%	7.4%	14.8%	18.5%	37.0%			
All	8	3	7	11	13	42	2.4	1.5
	19.0%	7.1%	16.7%	26.2%	31.0%			
Defense Attorneys								
Cities A & C	1	3	0	6	13	23	3.2	1.2
	4.3%	13.0%		26.1%	56.5%			
City B	3	1	5	4	26	39	3.3	1.2
	7.7%	2.6%	12.8%	10.3%	66.7%			
All	4	4	5	10	39	62	3.2	1.2
	6.5%	6.5%	8.1%	16.1%	62.9%			

greater number of compensation categories.[1] This was also true of defense attorneys who either were younger or spent a larger percentage of their worktime on criminal practice.[2]

When the composite scores were examined in the light of search and seizure perspective, police officers with a low reasonable-low productive profile had the highest average composite score in their sample. Since the police were least inclined to award many categories of compensation, it may be suggested that they had to see a greater percentage of searches as unreasonable and unproductive before they would be more liberal in the awarding of compensation.[3]

To discover what effect respondents felt the possession of contraband or incriminating evidence should have on an illegally searched suspect's ability to receive compensation, respondents were asked: "The fact that the person illegally searched possessed contraband or incriminating evidence should lessen the illegally searched person's eligibility for compensation" (*Possession Contraband Should Lessen Eligibility for Compensation*).

Table 10-3 reveals that police, with an overall mean continuum score of 68.6, and the district attorneys, with 71.5, considered that possession of contraband should lessen eligibility for compensation, while defense attorneys, with a mean score of 45.2, were somewhat of the opposite opinion. Interestingly, no correlation existed between responses to this question and composite compensation score.[4]

With the feeling established that illegally searched persons should be

Table 10-3
Possession of Contraband Should Lessen Eligibility for Compensation

	n	$\bar{x}$	s
Police			
City A	26	64.7	38.7
City B	67	70.1	32.7
All	93	68.6	34.3
District Attorneys			
Cities A and C	14	66.7	41.2
City B	28	73.8	27.5
All	42	71.5	32.4
Defense Attorneys			
Cities A and C	23	40.9	38.6
City B	40	47.6	34.7
All	63	45.2	36.0

compensated for some types of harm suffered, and the proviso that possession of contraband should lessen eligibility for compensation, the question arises as to who should pay that compensation. To see what support there was for payment of at least part of the compensation by the police officer in a given case, respondents were presented with the following statement:

A police officer should have to pay at least part of the monetary compensation himself (Please mark only one):
a.   In all cases
b.   Only when the violation was excessive
c.   Only when the violation was intentional
d.   When the violation was *either* excessive *or* intentional
e.   When the violation was *both* excessive *and* intentional
f.   In no case
g.   Other. Please explain _____.

(Payment of Compensation by Police Officers)

The focus in the question, it should be noted, passes from the harm suffered by the person illegally searched to the conduct of the offending officer.

As table 10-4 shows, forty-eight (51.1%) of the police officers felt that an officer should never pay compensation, thirty-three (35.1%) considered that partial payment should be paid by the officer when the violation was both excessive and intentional, and ten (10.6%) when it was intentional alone. When numerical values were attributed to the ordinal scale answers to this question, (with the values ranging from a low of 2.0 for a reply of "in no case" to a high of 7.0 for a response "in all cases,") it may be observed that the overall mean police response was 2.8.

District attorneys recorded an overall mean response of 3.1, with twenty

Table 10-4
Payment of Compensation by Police Officer

	A police officer should have to pay at least part of the monetary compensation himself:								
	All Cases	Excessive or Intentional Violations	Intentional Violations	Excessive Violations	Excessive and Intentional Violations	No Case	n	$\bar{x}$	s
Numerical Value of Category	(7)	(6)	(5)	(4)	(3)	(2)			
Police									
City A	0	1 3.8%	3 11.5%	0	6 23.1%	16 61.5%	26	2.7	1.2
City B	0	2 2.9%	7 10.3%	0	27 39.7%	32 47.1%	68	2.8	1.1
All	0	3 3.2%	10 10.6%	0	33 35.1%	48 51.1%	94	2.8	1.1
District Attorneys									
Cities A & C	1 6.7%	2 13.3%	1 6.7%	0	4 26.7%	7 46.7%	15	3.3	1.7
City B	1 3.6%	2 7.1%	1 3.6%	0	11 39.2%	13 46.4%	28	3.0	1.4
All	2 4.7%	4 9.3%	2 4.7%	0	15 34.9%	20 46.5%	43	3.1	1.5
Defense Attorneys									
Cities A & C	0	8 36.4%	1 4.5%	0	8 36.4%	5 22.7%	22	4.0	1.7
City B	3 7.7%	10 25.6%	5 12.8%	0	14 35.9%	7 17.9%	39	4.2	1.7
All	3 4.9%	18 29.5%	6 9.8%	0	22 36.1%	12 19.7%	61	4.1	1.7

(46.5%) considering that an officer should never pay compensation, fifteen (34.9%) deciding that he should when the violation was both excessive and intentional, and four (9.3%) that he should when the violation was either excessive or intentional.

Defense attorneys returned a mean response of 4.1, with twenty-two (36.1%) feeling that an officer should pay at least part of the compensation himself when the violation was both excessive and intentional, and eighteen (29.5%) when it was either excessive or intentional. Only twelve (19.7%) considered that an officer should never pay compensation. As might be expected, defense attorneys as a whole were more eager than district attorneys, who in turn were more eager than police officers, to see that police officers who violated Fourth Amendment rights should pay at least part of the compensation. There was a tendency in all samples for respondents who favored payment in a greater number of compensation categories to support payment by police officers in a greater number of cases.[5] Finally, defense attorneys who felt that possession of contraband or incriminating evidence should lessen the illegally searched person's eligibility for compensation were less inclined to favor payment of compensation by police officers.[6]

It has been suggested that an administrative board be set up to deal with questions of compensation for Fourth Amendment rights. When this issue was examined and an analysis undertaken of respondent reactions to the proposition that "An administrative board should be set up to deal with questions of compensation for the violation of Fourth Amendment rights" (*Establishment of Administrative Board for Questions of Compensation*), it was noted that there was very little support for this proposal. (See table 10-5.) While the police, with an overall mean score of 42.3, and the district attorneys, with one of 34.5, were somewhat against such a board, the defense attorneys, who had an overall mean of 51.3, were noncommittal. Prosecution and defense officials who had favored payment in more compensation categories or had been more eager for police officers to pay compensation showed stronger support.[7]

The lack of support for an administrative board would seem to suggest, in this area at least, a desire to work through the existing court structure. While there was overall support from all samples for the payment of some compensation depending upon the type of harm suffered, there was a general feeling that possession of contraband or incriminating evidence should lessen the illegally searched person's eligibility to receive compensation.

As a consequence of these reactions, the suggestion may be made that any unreasonable search and seizure should give rise to a prima facie cause of action for compensation. However, if the illegal search were productive, the prima facie cause of action would be rebutted. Hence, only in special circumstances would compensation be awarded when contraband or incriminating evidence was uncovered in an unreasonable search and seizure. Since there was little support for even partial payment of compensation by the offending police officer,

Table 10-5
Establishment of Administrative Board for Questions
of Compensation

	n	$\bar{x}$	s
Police			
City A	25	35.3	34.8
City B	68	44.9	36.0
All	93	42.3	35.8
District Attorneys			
Cities A and C	15	31.3	33.1
City B	30	36.1	31.8
All	45	34.5	31.9
Defense Attorneys			
Cities A and C	23	53.7	35.7
City B	40	50.0	35.2
All	63	51.3	35.1

responsibility for satisfying a court award would rest with the agency which employed the officer.

Departmental Action

Departmental action involves the internal disciplinary procedure a police department invokes against an officer who has transgressed its rules and regulations. In the context of search and seizure, it may be considered a means of punishing a police officer after a violation of Fourth Amendment rights has occurred, and of discouraging future violations by instituting internal disciplinary action. The procedure's potential deterrent effect would be strengthened by the issuance of detailed departmental regulations, to which its officers are expected to adhere. Unlike the question of compensation, the focus is on the police officer's actions rather than on the injury suffered.

Chapter nine indicated strong support for police involvement both in the issuance and enforcment of police rules of conduct in search and seizure: the suggestion that police departments should issue detailed search and seizure regulations was supported by the police, with a mean score of 66.9, the district attorneys with a mean of 76.6, and the defense attorneys, with a mean of 83.8.

To learn which types of unreasonable search and seizure situations were felt to require departmental action, we asked respondents:

Regardless of the availability of other procedures, a police officer who has violated a suspect's Fourth Amendment rights should have departmental action taken against him:

a. In all cases
b. Only when the violation was excessive
c. Only when the violation was intentional
d. When the violation was *either* excessive *or* intentional
e. When the violation was *both* excessive *and* intentional
f. In no case
g. Other. Please explain _____.

(*Use of Departmental Action*)

Table 10-6 reveals that forty-three (46.2%) police officers felt action should be taken when the violation was both excessive and intentional, twenty-seven (29.0%) in no case, and fourteen (15.1%) when the violation was intentional. When numerical values were given to the ordinal response categories, the overall mean police score was 3.3 on a scale from 2.0 to 7.0.

District attorneys returned an overall mean score of 3.9 with nineteen (44.2%) favoring departmental action for violations that were both excessive and intentional, eleven (25.6%) for violations that were either excessive or intentional, and six (14.0%) for violations that were intentional alone. Six (14.0%) were against departmental action in any case.

Defense attorneys recorded an overall mean score of 5.0. Twenty-nine (47.5%) advocated departmental action when the violation was either excessive or intentional, eighteen (29.5%) when the violation was both excessive and intentional, and six each (9.8%) favored action either when the violation was intentional or in all cases. Only two (3.3%) thought that departmental action should be undertaken in no case.

Respondents were in all cases more eager to invoke departmental action than they were to approve monetary compensation by a police officer. In all three samples, support for compensation by a police officer proved a good indicator of support for departmental action.[8] In no case, however, was any significant association found between desire for issuance of detailed departmental regulations and for invocation of departmental action.[9]

One feature apparent from table 10-6 is the tendency of all respondents in Cities A and C to favor greater use of departmental action. Interestingly, police officers with low reasonable-low productive search and seizure perspectives recorded the highest support for departmental action, while those with high reasonable-high productive perspectives showed the lowest.[10]

To explore the effect respondents felt the discovery of contraband or incriminating evidence should have on the question of discipline respondents were asked to register their agreement or disagreement with the statement: "The fact that the person illegally searched possessed contraband or incriminating evidence should lessen the likelihood of the police officer being disciplined" (*Possession Contraband Should Lessen Likelihood of Discipline*).

Table 10-6
Use of Departmental Action

Numerical Value of Category	All Cases (7)	Excessive or Intentional Violations (6)	Intentional Violations (5)	Excessive Violations (4)	Excessive and Intentional Violations (3)	No Case (2)	n	$\bar{x}$	s
Police									
City A	0	1 4.0%	9 36.0%	0	10 40.0%	5 20.0%	25	3.6	1.3
City B	2 2.9%	6 8.8%	5 7.4%	0	33 48.5%	22 32.4%	68	3.2	1.4
All	2 2.2%	7 7.5%	14 15.1%	0	43 46.2%	27 29.0%	93	3.3	1.3
District Attorneys									
Cities A & C	0	5 33.3%	3 20.0%	0	5 33.3%	2 13.3%	15	4.3	1.5
City B	0	6 21.4%	3 10.7%	1 3.6%	14 50.0%	4 14.3%	28	3.8	1.4
All	0	11 25.6%	6 14.0%	1 2.3%	19 44.2%	6 14.0%	43	3.9	1.5
Defense Attorneys									
Cities A & C	2 9.1%	14 63.6%	2 9.1%	0	3 13.6%	1 4.5%	22	5.4	1.3
City B	4 10.3%	15 38.5%	4 10.3%	0	15 38.5%	1 2.6%	39	4.7	1.6
All	6 9.8%	29 47.5%	6 9.8%	0	18 29.5%	2 3.3%	61	5.0	1.5

Regardless of the availability of other procedures, a police officer who has violated a suspect's Fourth Amendment rights should have departmental action taken against him:

As table 10-7 indicates, feelings about this proposition were mixed. Only police, with a mean continuum score of 68.0 were in favor of the proposition, while district attorneys, with a mean of 51.5, were ambivalent, and defense attorneys, with a mean of 37.3, were against it. These responses were correlated with those concerning departmental action. We found that district attorneys who felt strongly that possession of contraband by a suspect should lessen the likelihood that the police officer be disciplined, tended to be less supportive of the invocation of departmental action.[11] Similar negative but statistically insignificant correlations existed for police and defense samples.

A major criticism of internal discipline is that it tends to condone police conduct. Since the focus in internal discipline is on the conduct of the police officer, and not on the suspect, it might be argued that the fact that the illegally searched person possessed contraband or incriminating evidence should not affect the likelihood of the police officer being disciplined. In this way the protection of all suspects' Fourth Amendment rights would be preserved, a consideration which would assume even greater importance if the exclusionary rule were modified; for departmental action would still cover those cases in which the exclusionary rule would no longer operate.

Criminal Prosecution

Of all the proceedings that may be instituted against a police officer, criminal prosecution is regarded as the most serious, implying society's moral concern and, in the case of conviction, condemnation. In the context of search and seizure it may be considered as a means of punishing an officer who has violated a suspect's Fourth Amendment rights, and of discouraging future violations by making an example of the officer. As with departmental action, the focus is on the police officer's actions.

Table 10-7
Possession of Contraband Should Lessen Likelihood of Discipline

	n	$\bar{x}$	s
Police			
City A	26	60.8	38.7
City B	67	70.9	30.1
All	93	68.0	32.8
District Attorneys			
Cities A and C	14	44.9	37.7
City B	28	54.8	31.1
All	42	51.5	33.3
Defense Attorneys			
Cities A and C	23	41.8	35.7
City B	38	34.6	31.4
All	61	37.3	33.0

To identify unreasonable search and seizure situations which were felt to merit criminal prosecution, respondents were asked:

Regardless of the availability of other procedures, a police officer who has violated a suspect's Fourth Amendment rights should be criminally prosecuted:
a.   In all cases
b.   Only when the violation was excessive
c.   Only when the violation was intentional
d.   When the violation was *either* excessive *or* intentional
e.   When the violation was *both* excessive *and* intentional
f.   In no case
g.   Other. Please explaain _____.

(*Use of Criminal Prosecution*)

Table 10-8 reveals that there was little overall support for criminal prosecution. Forty-three (47.3%) police officers felt that criminal prosecution should occur in no case, thirty-five (38.5%) favored prosecution when the violation was both excessive and intentional, and ten (11.0%) when the violation was intentional alone. When numerical values were given, the overall mean police response was 2.8.

The district attorneys returned a mean score of 2.7, with twenty-four (57.1%) stating that an officer should never be criminally prosecuted, and thirteen (31.0%) advocating it only when the violation was both excessive and intentional. Defense attorneys, recording a mean response of 3.4, included twenty-five (43.9%) who advocated criminal prosecution when the violation was both excessive and intentional, eight (14.0%) only when it was intentional, and seven (12.3%) when it was either excessive or intentional. Fifteen (26.3%) believed that a police officer should not be criminally prosecuted in any case.

As might be expected, all respondents favored a far more limited use of criminal prosecution than of departmental action. Attitude toward departmental action was, however, a fairly good indicator of attitude toward criminal prosecution,[12] as indeed was also support for payment of compensation by a police officer.[13]

As with departmental action, respondents in Cities A and C were greater supporters of criminal prosecution than their counterparts in City B. When background variables were examined, it was noted that defense attorneys who had spent more years in practice were more eager advocates of the use of criminal sanctions.[14]

When it came to the question of whether "The fact that the person illegally searched possessed contraband or incriminating evidence should lessen the likelihood of the police officer being criminally prosecuted" (*Possession Contraband Lessen Likelihood of Criminal Prosecution*), both police, with an overall mean continuum score of 66.0 and prosecution officials, with one of 66.4, felt

Table 10-8
Invocation of Criminal Prosecution

	Regardless of the availability of other procedures, a police officer who has violated a suspect's Fourth Amendment rights should be criminally prosecuted:								
Numerical Value of Category	All Cases	Excessive or Intentional Violations	Intentional Violations	Excessive Violations	Excessive and Intentional Violations	No Case	n	x̄	s
	7	6	5	4	3	2			
Police									
City A	0	0	7 / 28.0%	1 / 4.0%	7 / 28.0%	10 / 40.0%	25	3.2	1.2
City B	0	2 / 3.0%	3 / 4.5%	0	28 / 42.4%	33 / 50.0%	66	2.7	.9
All	0	2 / 2.2%	10 / 11.0%	1 / 1.1%	35 / 38.5%	43 / 47.3%	91	2.8	1.1
Defense Attorneys									
Cities A & C	1 / 7.1%	0	2 / 14.3%	0	3 / 21.4%	8 / 57.1%	14	3.0	1.5
City B	0	0	1 / 3.6%	1 / 3.6%	10 / 35.7%	16 / 57.1%	28	2.5	.7
All	1 / 2.4%	0	3 / 7.1%	1 / 2.4%	13 / 31.0%	24 / 57.1%	42	2.7	1.1
Defense Attorneys									
Cities A & C	0	3 / 15.0%	4 / 20.0%	0	9 / 45.0%	4 / 20.0%	20	3.7	1.4
City B	0	4 / 10.8%	4 / 10.8%	2 / 5.4%	16 / 43.2%	11 / 29.7%	37	3.3	1.3
All	0	7 / 12.3%	8 / 14.0%	2 / 3.5%	25 / 43.9%	15 / 26.3%	57	3.4	1.3

Table 10-9

Possession of Contraband Should Lessen Likelihood of Criminal Prosecution

	n	$\bar{x}$	s
Police			
City A	26	58.5	42.2
City B	67	71.6	32.7
All	93	68.0	35.9
District Attorneys			
Cities A and C	13	54.5	39.4
City B	27	72.1	30.8
All	40	66.4	34.3
Defense Attorneys			
Cities A and C	22	47.5	37.1
City B	39	40.3	32.7
All	61	42.9	34.2

that it should, while defense attorneys, with a mean of 42.9, were of a somewhat contrary view. (See table 10-9.) Police who had been involved in a greater number of suppression hearings during the previous year, district attorneys who had spent longer in the district attorney's office, and defense attorneys who spent a lower percentage of their worktime on criminal practice in the previous year all felt more strongly that the likelihood of prosecution should be lessened.[15]

When responses were correlated with those on the use of criminal prosecution, it was found that only in the district attorney sample was there any significant association. District attorneys who felt more strongly that the likelihood of a police officer being prosecuted should be lessened by the suspect's possession of contraband or incriminating evidence, were at the same time less likely to favor criminal prosecution.[16]

Few respondents knew of any police officer being criminally prosecuted for an unreasonable search and seizure during the previous year. Only six (6.4%) police officers, two (4.4%) district attorneys, and five (7.8%) defense attorneys knew of such proceedings. These figures were too small to allow for comment on the relationship between awareness of such criminal prosecution and attitude toward its use.

There was little support, then, for much use of criminal prosecution, probably because it was considered too drastic a measure to invoke regularly. In addition, there was general support for the idea that possession of contraband or incriminating evidence should lessen the likelihood of the police officer being criminally prosecuted. Thus the responses suggest that criminal prosecution should be employed only when outrageous circumstances surround the unreasonable search and seizure. And even when outrageous circumstances have occurred, possession of contraband by the illegally searched suspect should be considered a factor which militates against prosecution.

Conclusion

The findings of this chapter indicate a firm desire for police departments to issue detailed regulations on search and seizure, and strong support for use of departmental action against an offending police officer. While reactions were mixed, a theoretical argument was advanced suggesting that possession of contraband should not lessen the likelihood of the police officer being disciplined.

On the issue of monetary compensation for illegally searched persons, respondents generally felt that some money should be forthcoming depending upon the type of harm suffered. However, respondents were against setting up an administrative board to deal with questions of compensation and in favor of the proposition that possession of contraband should lessen an illegally searched person's eligibility for compensation. There was little support for even partial payment of compensation by the offending police officer. Thus, responsibility for satisfying a court award would rest with the government agency which employs the officer, a result which would complement tighter internal administrative procedures.

Finally, it was felt that criminal prosecution was a measure that should be used only in outrageous circumstances, with possession of contraband by the illegally searched person constituting a factor which militates against its invocation.

Notes

1. The correlations were: composite compensation score and age, $-.30^*$; and years in law practice, $-.35^*$.

2. The correlations were: composite compensation score and age, $-.26^*$; and percentage work time spent on criminal practice, $.24^*$.

3. The relevant figures were:

Search and Seizure Perspective	n	$\bar{x}$	s
Low reasonable-low productive	18	2.2	1.6
Low reasonable-high productive	12	1.6	1.3
Medium reasonable-medium productive	24	1.7	1.4
High reasonable-low productive	18	1.7	1.2
High reasonable-high productive	20	1.5	1.4

4. The relevant correlations were: police, $r = -.02^{**}$; district attorneys, $r = .09^{**}$; defense attorneys, $r = -.10^{**}$.

5. The correlations were: ⅄45 for police, .29* for district attorneys and .38 for defense attorneys.

6. $r = -.35$.

7. The correlations for district attorneys were: *composite compensation score/Establishment of Administrative Board for Questions of Compensation*, .48; *Payment of Compensation by Police Officer/Establishment of Administrative Board for Questions of Compensation*, .38. The correlations for defense attorneys were .34 and .35, respectively. The correlations were insignificant in the police sample.

8. The relevant correlations were .53 for police, .62 for district attorneys, and .52 for defense attorneys.

9. The correlations were .14** for police, .02** for district attorneys and .08** for defense attorneys.

10. The relevant figures were:

Search and Seizure Perspective	Use of Departmental Action		
	n	$\overline{x}$	*s*
Low reasonable-low productive	18	4.1	1.6
Low reasonable-high productive	12	3.2	.9
Medium reasonable-medium productive	24	3.4	1.3
High reasonable-low productive	18	3.2	1.4
High reasonable-high productive	20	2.8	1.1

11. $r = -.47$.

12. The relevant correlations were .49 for police, .30* for district attorneys and .35 for defense attorneys.

13. The correlations between *Payment of Compensation by Police Officer* and *Use of Criminal Prosecution* were .43 for police, .53 for district attorneys and .48 for defense attorneys.

14. $r = .27*$.

15. The relevant correlations were .20 for police, .29* for district attorneys and −.29* for defense attorneys.

16. $r = -.42$. Similar negative but statistically insignificant correlations were found in the police and defense samples.

11 Summary and Conclusion

The primary objective of this study has been to examine police, prosecution, and defense perceptions of various aspects of the problem of protecting Fourth Amendment rights; to locate and examine areas of conflict; and to suggest what modifications might best be made to the present situation. The desired end is a framework that will better ensure the Fourth Amendment's guarantee against unreasonable search and seizure with the least overall cost to the interests of law enforcement. In this chapter such a framework will be presented, incorporating modifications suggested by the research findings, to improve the network of procedures designed to protect Fourth Amendment rights.

The theoretical framework of this study divided searches into those which are legally reasonable or unreasonable, and those which are productive or unproductive. As outlined earlier in figure 3-1, this subdivision gives rise to a two-by-two table in which four types of searches are depicted: (a) searches conducted in accordance with the Fourth Amendment which reveal contraband or incriminating evidence; (b) searches conducted in accordance with the Fourth Amendment which reveal neither contraband nor incriminating evidence; (c) searches conducted in violation of the Fourth Amendment which reveal contraband or incriminating evidence; and (d) searches conducted in violation of the Fourth Amendment which reveal neither contraband nor incriminating evidence.

It is, of course, only the latter two types of searches which police officers have to be deterred from making, and which give rise to the issues of compensation and discipline. The question to be answered concerns the changes that may, in view of the findings of this study, best be made in the present system of protecting Fourth Amendment rights.

The exclusionary rule is at present the primary mechanism for dealing with searches conducted in violation of the Fourth Amendment that reveal contraband or incriminating evidence. Numerous drawbacks to the rule were, however, noted in chapter two. Thus it has been argued that the rule frees the guilty, but does not compensate the innocent; that it does not punish or affect the errant police official; that the complexity of the law prevents a police officer from understanding the scope of his legal authority; that the rule is inflexible, sensitive neither to the seriousness of the violation nor the police motive involved; that it causes delay and diverts attention from the question of guilt or innocence; that it handcuffs the police and thus encourages police perjury, extrajudicial punishment, and immunization of criminals.

The main theoretical argument advanced at present by the Supreme Court for maintaining the exclusionary rule is based on the factual rationale. An examination of responses to the questions on deterrence, and an analysis of the factors associated with an officer's decision to search, as revealed in the reactions to the cases presented, showed that not only did the rule not deter in most circumstances, but when it did, it did so in a negative manner and on the basis of limited knowledge of the law. Moreover, the factor most highly associated with a police officer's decision to conduct a search was found to be his personal assessment of the situation as opposed to either his projection of the court's assessment or the frequency with which he saw the situation as occurring. Thus the findings of this study indicate no support for the retention of the rule on the grounds that it fulfills a positive deterrent function. Nor was there any support for keeping it on the grounds that it performs a disciplinary function.

Only on the basis of the normative rationale was there any argument for retaining the exclusionary rule. Both district and defense attorneys strongly supported the idea that the courts should not participate in illegal behavior by admitting the evidence obtained by it. While the police were ambivalent about the merits of the normative rationale, their objections appeared to relate not so much to the normative theoretical foundations of the rule as to the consequences of the way in which it is presently administered.

Indeed, when confronted with the choice of abolishing the rule, respondents did not choose this possibility, largely because they felt that the demands of the normative rationale militated against it. These demands were, however, apparently met to some extent by the proposed limitation to cover only willful and excessive violations of Fourth Amendment rights. Though this proposal by no means received direct resounding support, reactions to the cases indicated the desirability of some type of reorganization in the administration of the law so that the interests of law enforcement might be more fairly served. One way this could be achieved would be by limiting the exclusionary rule to cover only violations of the Fourth Amendment that are willful and excessive.

Such a modification would, indeed, appear to fulfill many of the conflicting needs revealed in this study. While law enforcement interests would be more adequately served, the requirements of the normative rationale would still be met to a considerable extent, and judicial input in formulating and overseeing police rules of conduct in search and seizure would be maintained. Limiting the exclusionary rule to cover only willful and excessive violations would give it greater potential as a deterrent, since it is more likely that willful and excessive searches can be discouraged, as opposed to searches which are only technically or accidentally unreasonable. Such a modification would also presumably lessen the police sensation of being handcuffed, and diminish the incidence of police perjury, and the extrajudicial punishment and immunization of criminals. It would certainly lessen the number of guilty persons allowed to go free as the result of police error, and put an end to the "universal 'capital punishment' "[1] which is presently being inflicted upon all illegally seized evidence.

Since fear was voiced that the police may feel, as a result of the rule's modification, that they enjoy greater license to search at will, implementation of this proposal would have to be accompanied by in-depth training. Indeed, an important finding of this study was the general desire for police involvement in both issuing and enforcing police rules of conduct in search and seizure. A need was voiced for police departments to issue detailed regulations and provide officers with adequate training. Since a police officer will apparently follow his own conscience in deciding whether to undertake a search, he should be presented with guidelines, and more importantly, be made fully aware of the spirit of those guidelines. Guidelines would also be particularly appropriate for recurring situations, since in both prosecution and defense samples frequency of occurrence of the situation was the strongest predictor of the action respondents believed would be undertaken on the streets.

As there was good support for departmental action against a police officer who had infringed an individual's Fourth Amendment rights, it would appear that wider and improved use of departmental action should be explored to deal with these violations. Seeing that the focus is on the conduct of the police officer and not on the illegally searched individual, departmental action would be invoked even if the search uncovered contraband or incriminating evidence. With police departments issuing detailed regulations, providing adequate training, and seeing to the enforcement of the regulations, a tight internal administrative system might be developed. To counteract outside distrust of internal police review, complaints could be actively encouraged, rather than discouraged; all complaints could be accepted initially, and investigative work performed by special internal units; all hearings could be open to the public, with quasi-judicial procedures followed and decisions fully publicized.[2]

Compensation is the one method which can provide an illegally searched individual with monetary as well as psychological satisfaction for the infringement of his rights. Depending upon the type of harm suffered, respondents generally felt that those who had been illegally searched should receive some form of compensation. Since, however, they did not approve setting up an administrative board to deal with questions of compensation, redress would continue to be through civil action in state or federal court. Seeing that there was a general feeling that possession of contraband or incriminating evidence should lessen the illegally searched person's eligibility to receive compensation, it may be suggested that any unreasonable search and seizure should give rise to a prima facie cause of action for compensation. If, however, the illegal search were productive, the prima facie cause of action would be rebutted, and the claimant would have to show the existence of special circumstances in order to obtain an award of damages. Hence only in special circumstances, such as a violation resulting in severe injuries, or a police officer shown to be motivated by malice toward the claimant, would compensation be awarded when evidence was discovered.

To improve the viability of these actions it has been proposed that special jury instructions be created, or jury use abolished, that minimum fixed damages be established, that successful claimants be paid reasonable attorney fees, and that the employing agency be made liable for the wrongful actions of its officials. This last proposal is well supported by our finding that few respondents favored even partial payment of compensation by an offending officer. Placing the responsibility for satisfying a court award with the agency that employs the officer would be consistent with the recommended tighter internal administrative structure.

Criminal prosecution of a police officer for violating Fourth Amendment rights is at present seldom invoked. In view of the serious nature of this measure, and the fact that respondents considered it should be instituted only in outrageous circumstances, we do not suggest it be employed on a wider basis.

Returning now to the theoretical framework, we can see that the population of unreasonable searches and seizures can be divided into unreasonable searches which are willful and excessive and those which are not. Remedies available to an illegally searched person, and actions that may be instituted against an offending police officer would depend upon the category of unreasonable search involved. As can be seen from figure 11-1, if the search were willful and excessive, and revealed contraband or incriminating evidence, departmental action could be taken against the offending officer, and if outrageous circumstances surrounded the violation, he could also be subjected to criminal prosecution. The illegally seized evidence would be excluded in the criminal

	Search Legally Reasonable		
	Yes	No	
		Violation Willful and Excessive	
		Yes	No
Yes		Evidence excluded	—
		Departmental action	Departmental action
		Compensation in special circumstances	Compensation in special circumstances
		Criminal prosecution in outrageous circumstances	—
Evidence Found			
No		Departmental action	Departmental action
		Compensation	Compensation
		Criminal prosecution in outrageous circumstances	—

Figure 11-1. Proposed Availability of Procedures and Actions

action against the suspect, and if special circumstances existed he would be eligible to receive compensation for the harm suffered.

If the search were willful and excessive, but did not produce contraband or incriminating evidence, departmental action and, in outrageous circumstances, criminal prosecution could be instituted against the officer. An action for compensation would be available on a wide basis for the illegally searched individual.

If the search were not willful and excessive, but produced contraband or incriminating evidence, departmental action could be instituted against the police officer, and in special circumstances compensation awarded. However, the evidence would be admitted at the trial of the illegally searched suspect. Finally, if the search were not willful and excessive and did not uncover contraband or incriminating evidence, departmental action could be taken against the offending officer and an action for compensation would be available for the illegally searched individual.

These proposals are not radical. They are changes that combine the views of police, prosecution, and defense officials with the writings of scholars, the dicta of judges, and the proposals of legislators. Much will depend upon the ability of the police to police themselves, although the limited retention of court involvement in the overseeing of police rules should provide the impetus for the police authorities to follow the desired course of action.

In sum, by instituting strong, visible internal police administrative procedures, by limiting the application of the exclusionary rule, and by making both the civil action for compensation and criminal prosecution viable measures in the appropriate circumstances, it is hoped that a structure for the protection of Fourth Amendment rights would be established that would better accommodate the interests of both law enforcement and civil liberties.

Notes

1. *Bivens* v. *Six Unknown Named Agents of Federal Bureau of Narcotics* 403 U.S. 388, 419 (1971). (Burger, C.J., dissenting.)

2. "Grievance Response Mechanisms for Police Misconduct," *Virginia Law Review* 55 (1969):936-937.

Appendix A
Reliability: The Internal Consistency of the Research Instrument

The four items employed to test the internal consistency of the measuring instrument were:

1. The exclusionary rule should be abolished (*Abolition of Rule*).
2. Reliable physical evidence should be admitted in criminal prosecutions regardless of the methods used in obtaining it (*Admission of All Evidence*).
3. A suspect who has been illegally searched should have the illegally seized evidence excluded in court (*Evidence Should Be Excluded*).
4. It would be improper for the courts to admit any illegally seized evidence because they would be approving illegal conduct (*Impropriety of Admitting Evidence*).

The first item calls for a simple choice concerning abolition, and *Admission of All Evidence* suggests the desirability of the major direct effect of abolition. But a near perfect correlation between these items would not be expected; for, though complementary, they are not identical. Thus while most respondents might be expected to give similar responses to the two questions, an individual might want abolition of the exclusionary rule, but at the same time feel that not all reliable physical evidence should be admitted regardless of the methods used in obtaining it. Alternatively he might favor the introduction of all reliable physical evidence, but feel that other factors, such as the courts' regular overseeing of police conduct, militate against abolition. Likewise, *Evidence Should Be Excluded* and *Impropriety of Admitting Evidence* tap similar aspects of the normative rationale (and we would expect similar attitudes to be held with regard to both items), but an individual who felt that an illegally searched person should be compensated by having the evidence excluded in court might not necessarily consider it improper for the courts to admit illegally seized evidence.

When appropriate statistical tests were performed, the correlation between *Abolition of Rule* and *Admission of All Evidence* turned out to be .55 for police, .72 for district attorneys and .81 for defense attorneys, as can be seen from table A-1. The corresponding correlations between *Evidence Should Be Excluded* and *Impropriety of Admitting Evidence* were .61, .48, and .50, respectively.

Since *Abolition of Rule* and *Admission of All Evidence* sought attitudes on abolition and *Evidence Should Be Excluded* and *Impropriety of Admitting*

Table A-1
Intercorrelations of Items Used to Measure the Reliability of
the Questionnaire

	Abolition of Rule	Admission of All Evidence	Evidence Should Be Excluded	Impropriety of Admitting Evidence
		Police		
Abolition of Rule	–	.55	–.52	–.59
		(93)[a]	(93)	(93)
		.001[b]	.001	.001
Admission of All Evidence		–	–.41	–.46
			(94)	(91)
			.001	.001
Evidence Should Be Excluded			–	.61
				(91)
				.001
Impropriety of Admitting Evidence				–
		District Attorneys		
Abolition of Rule	–	.72	–.71	–.42
		(45)	(45)	(45)
		.001	.001	.002
Admission of All Evidence		–	–.70	–.39
			(45)	(45)
			.001	.004
Evidence Should Be Excluded			–	.48
				(45)
				.001
Impropriety of Admitting Evidence				–
		Defense Attorneys		
Abolition of Rule	–	.81	–.60	–.73
		(64)	(64)	(64)
		.001	.001	.001
Admission of All Evidence		–	–.66	–.52
			(64)	(64)
			.001	.001
Evidence Should Be Excluded			–	.50
				(64)
				.001
Impropriety of Admitting Evidence				–

[a]Number of respondents.
[b]Level of significance.

Evidence feelings about retaining the rule on the basis of the normative rationale, negative correlations would be expected between *Abolition of Rule* and the two normative-retention propositions *Evidence Should Be Excluded* and *Impropriety of Admitting Evidence*, and between *Admission of All Evidence* and the two normative-retention propositions. Table A-1 shows that the hypothesized relationships did in fact hold true. While the police recorded correlations of $-.52$ and $-.59$ between *Abolition of Rule* and the two normative-retention questions, they registered correlations of $-.41$ and $-.46$ between *Admission of All Evidence* and those two items. The respective correlations were $-.71$, $-.42$, $-.70$ and $-.39$ for district attorneys and $-.60$, $-.73$, $-.66$ and $-.52$ for defense attorneys. When absolute values of the correlations between the four propositions were examined, the mean correlation in the police sample was .52, while it was .57 for district attorneys and .64 for defense attorneys.

Appendix B
Breakdown of
Background Variables

Police	Sex			Race		
	Male	*Female*		*White*	*Black*	*Other*
City A	28	0		28	0	0
	100%			100%		
City B	67	0		62	2	1
	100%			95.4%	3.1%	1.5%
All	95	0		90	2	1
	100%			96.7%	2.2%	1.1%

Police	Years on Force					
	0-2	*3-5*	*6-10*	*11-15*	*16-20*	*Over 20*
City A	4	1	5	8	5	2
	16.0%	4.0%	20.0%	32.0%	20.0%	8.0%
City B	1	10	27	12	6	11
	1.5%	14.9%	40.3%	17.9%	9.0%	16.4%
All	5	11	32	20	11	13
	5.4%	12.0%	34.8%	21.7%	12.0%	14.1%

Police	Number of Warrantless Felony and Misdemeanor Arrests Made During the Past Year					
	0	*1-3*	*4-10*	*11-20*	*21-30*	*Over 30*
City A	2	3	5	2	4	6
	9.1%	13.6%	22.7%	9.1%	18.2%	27.3%
City B	6	7	9	12	12	21
	9.0%	10.4%	13.4%	17.9%	17.9%	31.3%
All	8	10	14	14	16	27
	9.0%	11.2%	15.7%	15.7%	18.0%	30.3%

Police	Number of Suppression Hearings Involved in During the Past Year					
	0	*1-3*	*4-10*	*11-20*	*21-30*	*Over 30*
City A	14	6	3	0	0	0
	60.9%	26.1%	13.0%			
City B	20	14	15	14	2	1
	30.3%	21.2%	22.7%	21.2%	3.0%	1.5%
All	34	20	18	14	2	1
	38.2%	22.5%	20.2%	15.7%	2.2%	1.1%

Police						
				Work Described as Primarily		
	Patrol	*Investiga-tion*	*Supervi-sion/ Admini-stration*	*Patrol/ Investi-gation*	*Patrol/ Supervi-sion/Admi-nistration*	*Patrol/ Investiga-tion/Su-pervision/ Administra-tion*
City A	16	2	6	0	1	0
	64.0%	8.0%	9.0%		4.0%	
City B	30	21	9	6	0	1
	44.8%	31.3%	13.4%	9.0%		1.5%
All	46	23	15	6	1	1
	50.0%	25.0%	16.3%	6.5%	1.1%	1.1%

Police						
			Ever Worked on			
	Narcotics Squad		*Gambling Squad*		*Tactical Task Force*	
	Yes	*No*	*Yes*	*No*	*Yes*	*No*
City A	11	11	8	13	4	15
	50.0%	50.0%	38.1%	61.9%	21.1%	78.9%
City B	11	26	22	19	40	13
	29.7%	70.3%	53.7%	46.3%	75.5%	24.5%
All	22	37	30	32	44	28
	37.3%	62.7%	48.4%	51.6%	61.1%	38.9%

District Attorneys					
	Sex		*Race*		
	Male	*Female*	*White*	*Black*	*Other*
Cities A & C	14	1	14	0	0
	93.3%	6.7%	100%		
City B	28	2	27	2	0
	93.3%	6.7%	93.1%	6.9%	
All	42	3	41	2	0
	93.3%	6.7%	95.3%	4.7%	

District Attorneys					
	Age				
	Under 25	*25-34*	*35-44*	*45-54*	*Over 54*
Cities A & C	0	13	2	0	0
		86.7%	13.3%		
City B	1	22	3	3	0
	3.4%	75.9%	10.3%	10.3%	
All	1	35	5	3	0
	2.3%	79.5%	11.4%	6.8%	

District Attorneys						
	Years in District Attorney's Office					
	0-2	*3-5*	*6-10*	*11-15*	*16-20*	*Over 20*
Cities A & C	12	3	0	0	0	0
	80.0%	20.0%				
City B	17	10	3	0	0	0
	56.7%	33.3%	10.0%			
All	29	13	3	0	0	0
	64.4%	28.9%	6.7%			

District Attorneys	Number of Suppression Hearings Handled during the Last Year:					
	0	1-3	4-10	11-20	21-30	Over 30
Cities A & C	1	7	3	3	1	0
	6.7%	46.7%	20.0%	20.0%	6.7%	
City B	6	7	7	4	3	3
	20.0%	23.3%	23.3%	13.3%	10.0%	10.0%
All	7	14	10	7	4	3
	15.6%	31.1%	22.2%	15.6%	8.9%	6.7%

District Attorneys	Total Years in Law Practice					
	0-2	3-5	6-10	11-15	16-20	Over 20
Cities A & C	7	5	1	2	0	0
	46.7%	33.3%	6.7%	13.3%		
City B	16	6	3	3	1	1
	53.3%	20.0%	10.0%	10.0%	3.3%	3.3%
All	23	11	4	5	1	1
	51.1%	24.4%	8.9%	11.1%	2.2%	2.2%

District Attorneys	Ever Worked			
	As Private Defense Attorney		In Public Defender's Office	
	Yes	No	Yes	No
Cities A & C	7	8	2	12
	46.7%	53.3%	14.3%	85.7%
City B	9	21	1	29
	30.0%	70.0%	3.3%	96.7%
All	16	29	3	41
	35.6%	64.4%	6.8%	93.2%

Defense Attorneys	Sex		Race		
	Male	Female	White	Black	Other
Cities A & C	22	1	23	0	0
	95.7%	4.3%	100%		
City B	40	1	37	4	0
	97.6%	2.4%	90.2%	9.8%	
All	62	2	60	4	0
	96.9%	3.1%	93.8%	6.2%	

Defense Attorneys	Age				
	Under 25	25-34	35-44	45-54	Over 54
Cities A & C	0	13	4	4	1
		59.1%	18.2%	18.2%	4.5%
City B	0	14	19	6	2
		34.1%	46.3%	14.6%	4.9%
All	0	27	23	10	3
		42.9%	36.5%	15.9%	4.8%

Defense Attorneys	Total Years in Law Practicc					
	0-2	*3-5*	*6-10*	*11-15*	*16-20*	*Over 20*
Cities A & C	0	9	6	4	2	2
		39.1%	26.1%	17.4%	8.7%	8.7%
City B	4	4	11	11	6	5
	9.8%	9.8%	26.8%	26.8%	14.6%	12.2%
All	4	13	17	15	8	7
	6.3%	20.3%	26.6%	23.4%	12.5%	10.9%

Defense Attorneys	Percentage of Present Worktime Spent on Criminal Practice	
	$\overline{x}$	*s*
Cities A & C	43.1	23.3
City B	61.9	21.7
All	55.0	23.9

Defense Attorneys	Number of Suppression Hearings Handled during the Last Year:					
	0	*1-3*	*4-10*	*11-20*	*21-30*	*Over 30*
Cities A & C	4	7	6	3	1	1
	18.2%	31.8%	27.3%	13.6%	4.5%	4.5%
City B	0	5	18	13	3	2
		12.2%	43.9%	31.7%	7.3%	4.9%
All	4	12	24	16	4	3
	6.3%	19.0%	38.1%	25.4%	6.3%	4.8%

Defense Attorneys	Ever worked in			
	District Attorney's Office		Public Defender's Office	
	Yes	*No*	*Yes*	*No*
Cities A & C	9	14	7	14
	39.1%	60.9%	33.3%	66.7%
City B	10	30	8	31
	25.0%	75.0%	20.5%	79.5%
All	19	44	15	45
	30.2%	69.8%	25.0%	75.0%

Defense Attorneys	If Currently Working in a Public Defender's Office					
No. of Years	*0-2*	*3-5*	*6-10*	*11-15*	*16-20*	*Over 20*
Cities A & C	3	1	1	0	0	0
City B	2	1	2	0	0	0
All	5	2	3	0	0	0

			Ever a Private Defense Attorney	
	Full time	*Part time*	*Yes*	*No*
Cities A & C	0	5	5	0
City B	4	0	3	2
All	4	5	8	2

Bibliography

Research Methodology

Andreasen, Alan R. "Personalizing Mail Questionnaire Correspondence." *Public Opinion Quarterly* 34 (1970):273-277.

Bauer, Rainald K. "Structures of Mail Questionnaires: Test of Alternatives." *Public Opinion Quarterly* 27 (1963):307-311.

Blalock, Hubert M., Jr. *Social Statistics*. New York: McGraw-Hill Book Company, 1972.

Dillman, Don A. "Increasing Mail Questionnaire Response in Large Samples of the General Public." *Public Opinion Quarterly* 36 (1972):254-257.

Dillman, Don A.; Carpenter, Edwin H.; Christenson, James A.; and Brooks, Ralph M. "Increasing Mail Questionnaire Response: A Four State Comparison." *American Sociological Review* 39 (1974):744-756.

Gullahorn, John T., and Gullahorn, Jeanne E. "Increasing Returns From Non-Respondents." *Public Opinion Quarterly* 23 (1959):119-121.

_____ . "An Investigation of the Effects of Three Factors on Response to Mail Questionnaires." *Public Opinion Quarterly* 27 (1963):294-296.

Jahoda, M.; Deutsch, M.; and Cook, Stuart W. *Research Methods in Social Relations*. New York: Dryden Press, 1951.

Kerlinger, Fred N. and Pedhazur, Elazar J. *Multiple Regression in Behavioral Research*. New York: Holt Rinehart and Winston, 1973.

Levine, Sol and Gordon, Gerald. "Maximizing Returns on Mail Questionnaires." *Public Opinion Quarterly* 22 (1958-59):568-575.

Magnusson, David. *Test Theory*. Reading, Mass.: Addison-Wesley Publishing Company, 1966.

Mason, Ward S.; Dressel, Robert J.; and Bain, Robert K. "An Experimental Study of Factors Affecting Response to a Mail Survey of Beginning Teachers." *Public Opinion Quarterly* 25 (1961):296-299.

Nichols, Robert C. and Meyer, Mary Alice. "Timing Postcard Follow-ups in Mail Questionnaire Surveys." *Public Opinion Quarterly* 30 (1966):306-307.

Nie, Norman H.; Bent, Dale H.; and Hull, C. Hadlai. *Statistical Package for the Social Sciences*. New York: McGraw-Hill Book Company, 1970.

Nie, Norman H.; Hull, C. Hadlai; Jenkins, Jean G.; Steinbrenner, Karin; and Bent, Dale H. *Statistical Package for the Social Sciences*. Second Edition. New York: McGraw-Hill Book Company, 1975.

Nunnally, Jum C., Jr. *Introduction to Psychological Measurement*. New York: McGraw-Hill Book Company, 1970.

Oppenheim, Abraham Naftali. *Questionnaire Design and Attitude Measurement*. New York: Basic Books, 1966.

Parsons, Robert J. and Medford, Thomas S. "The Effect of Advance Notice in

Mail Surveys of Homogeneous Groups." *Public Opinion Quarterly* 36 (1972):254-255.

Payne, Stanley L. *The Art of Asking Questions.* Princeton, N.J.: Princeton University Press, 1951.

Pearlin, Leonard I. "The Appeals of Anonymity in Questionnaire Response." *Public Opinion Quarterly* 25 (1961):640-647.

Roeher, G. Allan. "Effective Techniques in Increasing Response to Mailed Questionnaires." *Public Opinion Quarterly* 27 (1963):299-302.

Simon, Julian L. *Basic Research Methods in Social Science.* New York: Random House, 1969.

Search and Seizure Literature

The Advocates. *Should Courts Admit Evidence that Police Have Seized Illegally?* Boston: WGBH Educational Foundation, 1974.

AELE Law Enforcement Legal Defense Center. *Survey of Police Misconduct Litigation 1967-1971.* Evanston, Ill.: Americans for Effective Law Enforcement, 1974.

Alberta, Mark E. and Werhan, Keith M. "A Federal Cause of Action Against a Municipality for Fourth Amendment Violations by its Agents." *George Washington Law Review* 42 (1974):850-868.

Allen, Francis A. "The Exclusionary Rule in the American Law of Search and Seizure." *Journal of Criminal Law, Criminology and Police Science* 52 (1961): 246-254.

The American Law Institute. *A Model Code of Pre-Arraignment Procedure: Proposed Official Draft.* Philadelphia: The American Law Institute, 1975.

Amsterdam, Anthony G. "Perspectives on the Fourth Amendment." *Minnesota Law Review* 58 (1974):349-477.

_____ . "Supreme Court and the Rights of Suspects in Criminal Cases." *New York University Law Review* 45 (1970):785-815.

Andenaes, Johannes. *Punishment and Deterrence.* Ann Arbor: University of Michigan Press, 1974.

Barton, Peter B. "Civilian Review Boards and the Handling of Complaints Against the Police." *University of Toronto Law Journal* 20 (1970):448-469.

Bennett, Fred Gilbert. "Judicial Integrity and Judicial Review: An Argument for Expanding the Scope of the Exclusionary Rule." *UCLA Law Review* 20 (1973):1129-1164.

Berner, Bruce G. "Search and Seizure: Status and Methodology." *Valparaiso University Law Review* 8 (1974):471-583.

Billy, Michael, Jr. and Rehnborg, Gordon A., Jr. "The Fourth Amendment Exclusionary Rule: Past, Present, No Future." *The American Criminal Law Review* 12 (1975):507-537.

Blalock, Joyce. *Civil Liability of Law Enforcement Officials.* Springfield, Ill.: Charles C. Thomas, 1974.

Blumrosen, Alfred W. "Contempt of Court and Unlawful Police Action." *Rutgers Law Review* 11 (1957):526-548.

Bogomolny, R.L. "Street Patrol: The Decision to Stop a Citizen." *Criminal Law Bulletin* 12 (1976):544-582.

Boker, Alys Rae and Corrigan, Carol A. "Making the Constable Culpable: A Proposal to Improve the Exclusionary Rule." *Hastings Law Journal* 27 (1976):1291-1303.

Call, Wayne W. "Money Damages for Unconstitutional Searches: Compensation or Deterrence? *Bivens* v. *Federal Bureau of Narcotics* (276 F. Supp 12). *Utah Law Review* (1972):276-282.

Canon, Bradley C. "Is the Exclusionary Rule in Failing Health? Some New Data and a Plea Against a Precipitous Conclusion." *Kentucky Law Journal* 62 (1974):681-730.

Carleton, Richard Douglas. "Constitutional Law—Search and Seizure: Federal Cause of Action for an Illegal Search and Seizure." *Duquesne Law Review* 10 (1972):710-716.

Caruso, David A. "After *United States* v. *Robinson*: Effect on New York Law." *Albany Law Review* 39 (1975):895-912.

Chevigny, Paul G. "Police Abuses in Connection with the Law of Search and Seizure." *Criminal Law Bulletin* 5 (1969):3-33.

_____. *Police Power: Police Abuses in New York City.* New York: Vintage Books, 1969.

Coe, Philip S. "The ALI Substantiality Test: A Flexible Approach to the Exclusionary Sanction." *Georgia Law Review* 10 (1975):1-51.

Colleli, Ralph J., Jr. "Warrantless Arrests by Police Survive a Constitutional Challenge." *The American Criminal Law Review* 14 (1976):193-216.

"Constitutional Law—Damages: Unreasonable Search by Federal Agents Under Color of Authority Provides a Federal Cause of Action for Damages Under the Fourth Amendment." *Brooklyn Law Review* 38 (1971):522-531.

"Constitutional Law—Federal Agents Conducting Unreasonable Searches and Seizures are Liable for Damages Under the Fourth Amendment." *Texas Law Review* 50 (1972):798-806.

"Constitutional Law—Fourth Amendment: Violation of Fourth Amendment by Federal Agents Gives Rise to a Cause for Action for Damages." *Alabama Law Review* 24 (1971):131-145.

"Constitutional Law—Searches and Seizures: Fourth Amendment Does Not Establish a Federal Cause of Action for Damages Caused by an Unreasonable Search and Seizure." *Harvard Law Review* 83 (1970):684-690.

Conway, Leo John. "The Plight of the Policeman—or a Case Against the Paradoxical Exclusionary Rule." *Capital University Law Review* 4 (1975):193-202.

Cox, William J. "The Decline of the Exclusionary Rule: An Alternative to Injustice." *Southwestern University Law Review* 4 (1972):68-91.

Davidow, Robert P. "Criminal Procedure Ombudsman as a Substitute for the Exclusionary Rule: A Proposal." *Texas Tech Law Review* 4 (1973):317-340.

Dellinger, Walter E. "Of Rights and Remedies: The Constitution as a Sword." *Harvard Law Review* 85 (1972):1532-1564.

Diamond, Harry. *Readings in Arrest, Search, and Seizure.* Los Angeles: Department of Police Science and Administration, Los Angeles State College, 1963.

Edwards, Richard A. "Criminal Liability for Unreasonable Searches and Seizures." *Virginia Law Review* 41 (1955):621-632.

"Effect of *Mapp* v. *Ohio* on Police Search and Seizure Practices in Narcotics Cases." *Columbia Journal of Law and Social Problems* 4 (1968):87-104.

Elrod, Joseph E., III. "Federal Jurisdiction—Suits Against Federal Officers for Violation of the Fourth Amendment." *North Carolina Law Review* 48 (1970):705-713.

"Excluding the Exclusionary Rule: Congressional Assault on *Mapp* v. *Ohio.*" *Georgetown Law Journal* 61 (1973):1453-1472.

"Exclusionary Rule: A Panel (Simon, Webb, Santarelli, Flynn)." *Federal Rules Decisions* 61 (1974):259-286.

"Federal Injunctive Relief from Illegal Search." *Washington University Law Quarterly* 1967 (1967):104-112.

Fine, Peter. "Private Assumption of the Police Function Under the Fourth Amendment." *Boston University Law Review* 51 (1971):464-482.

Finzen, Bruce A. "The Exclusionary Rule in Search and Seizure: Examination and Prognosis." *Kansas Law Review* 20 (1972):768-790.

Foote, Caleb. "Tort Remedies for Police Violations of Individual Rights." *Minnesota Law Review* 39 (1955):493-516.

Friedman, Gary. "The Impact of *Mapp* v. *Ohio* on Fairfield County." *Connecticut Bar Journal* 40 (1966):118-132.

Geller, W. "Enforcing the Fourth Amendment: The Exclusionary Rule and its Alternatives." *Washington University Law Quarterly* (1975):621-722.

Gibbons, John J. "Practical Prophylaxis and Appellate Methodology: The Exclusionary Rule as a Case Study in the Decisional Process." *Seton Hall Law Review* 3 (1972):295-322.

Gilligan, Francis A. "Attack the Probable Cause Equation." *Military Law Review* 65 (1974):115-131.

_____. "The Federal Tort Claims Act—An Alternative to the Exclusionary Rule." *The Journal of Criminal Law and Criminology* 66 (1975):1-22.

Goldberg, N.E. and Hartman, N. "The Suppression of the Exclusionary Rule." *National Legal Aid and Defender Association Briefcase* 32 (1974):79-82.

Gould, David S. "Use of § 1983 to Remedy Unconstitutional Police Conduct:

Guarding the Guards." *Harvard Civil Rights-Civil Liberties Law Review* 5 (1970): 104-120.

"Grievance Response Mechanisms for Police Misconduct." *Virginia Law Review* 55 (1969):909-951.

Grove, Daniel G. "Suppression of Illegally Obtained Evidence: The Standing Requirement on its Last Leg." *Catholic University Law Review* 18 (1968):150-179.

Gunter, Michael. "The Exclusionary Rule in Context." *North Carolina Law Review* 50 (1972):1049-1079.

Hornstein, Harvey A.; Bunker, Barbara Benedict; Burke, W. Warner; Gindes, Marion; and Lewicki, Roy J. *Social Intervention.* New York: The Free Press, 1971.

Horowitz, Edward J. "Excluding the Exclusionary Rule—Can There be an Effective Alternative?" *Los Angeles Bar Bulletin* 47 (1972):91-124.

Hudson, James R. "Police Review Boards and Police Accountability." *Law and Contemporary Problems* 36 (1971):515-538.

"Illegally Obtained Evidence Suppressed at Trial May Be Used in Sentencing Where Evidence is Reliable and Not Gathered to Influence the Sentencing Judge." *Columbia Law Review* 71 (1971):1102-1112.

Irons, Robert S. "The Burger Court: Discord in Search and Seizure." *University of Richmond Law Review* 8 (1974):433-445.

Isaacs, Paul F. "A Recent Assault on the Barricade Against Police Intrusion: The Exclusionary Rule." *Kentucky Bar Journal* 38 (1974):46-55.

Israel, Jerold H. and LaFave, Wayne R. *Criminal Procedure in a Nutshell.* St. Paul, Minn.: West Publishing Company, 1971.

Joest, David. "The Impeachment Exception: Decline of the Exclusionary Rule?" *Indiana Law Review* 8 (1975):865-889.

Jones, D.J., Jr. "Constitutional Law—Illegal Search and Seizure: Injunction." *North Carolina Law Review* 45 (1967):518-524.

Kaplan, John. "The Limits of the Exclusionary Rule." *Stanford Law Review* 26 (1974):1027-1055.

Katz, Michael. "The Supreme Court and the States: An Inquiry into *Mapp* v. *Ohio* in North Carolina. The Model, the Study and the Implications." *North Carolina Law Review* 45 (1966):119-151.

Keefe, Joseph F. "Contesting Searches and Seizures After the 1972-1974 Terms of the United States Supreme Court." *Connecticut Bar Journal* 49 (1975):45-76.

Keidser, Jill. "Nonusable Amounts of Narcotics: The Residual Dilemma." *Southwestern University Law Review* 6 (1974):224-234.

Korman, Edward R. "A Proposal to Modify the Exclusionary Rule." *New York Law Journal* 175, no. 62 (1976):1-2.

Kornfeld, Joseph A. "A Lawful Custodial Arrest for a Traffic Violation Justifies a Full Search of the Arrestee." *Houston Law Review* 11 (1974):1283-1293.

LaFave, Wayne R. " 'Case by Case Adjudication' versus 'Standardized Procedures.' The Robinson Dilemma." *The Supreme Court Review*
(1974):127-163.

———. "Improving Police Performance Through the Exclusionary Rule—Part
I: Current Police and Local Court Practices." *Missouri Law Review* 30
(1965):391-458.

———. "Improving Police Performance Through the Exclusionary Rule—Part
II: Defining the Norms and Training the Police." *Missouri Law Review* 30
(1965):566-610.

———. "Search and Seizure. 'The Course of True Law . . . Has Not . . . Run
Smooth.' " *University of Illinois Law Forum* (1966):255-389.

LaPrade, Carter. "An Alternative to the Exclusionary Rule Presently Administered Under the Fourth Amendment." *Connecticut Bar Journal* 48
(1974):100-110.

LaRussa, Dennis A. "Constitutional Law—Federal Civil Remedies: Implied Cause
of Action for Fourth Amendment Violations." *Tulane Law Review* 46
(1972):816-822.

Lee, Robert E., IV. "Constitutional Law—Search and Seizure: Search Incident to
a Lawful Custodial Arrest." *Mercer Law Review* 25 (1974):943-955.

Levin, Harvey Robert. "An Alternative to the Exclusionary Rule for Fourth
Amendment Violations." *Judicature* 58 (1974):74-80.

Little, Charles Dean. "The Exclusionary Rule of Evidence as a Means of
Enforcing Fourth Amendment Morality on Police." *Indiana Legal Forum* 3
(1970):375-412.

Lockhart, William B.; Kamisar, Yale; and Choper, Jesse H. *Constitutional Rights
and Liberties.* St. Paul, Minn.: West Publishing Company, 1970.

Maguire, R.F. "How to Unpoison the Fruit—The Fourth Amendment and the
Exclusionary Rule." *Journal of Criminal Law, Criminology and Police
Science* 55 (1964):307-321.

McGarr, Frank J. "The Exclusionary Rule: An Ill Conceived and Ineffective
Remedy." *Journal of Criminal Law, Criminology and Police Science* 52
(1961):266-270.

McGowan, Carl. "Rule Making and the Police." *Michigan Law Review* 70
(1972):659-694.

McKay, R.B. "*Mapp* v. *Ohio*, the Exclusionary Rule and the Right of Privacy."
Arizona Law Review 15 (1973):327-341.

Mello, Barbara. "Exclusionary Rule Under Attack." *Baltimore Law Review* 4
(1974):89-124.

Michigan Institute for Community Development and Services. *Arrest, Search and
Seizure Telephonic Lecture Series—Proceedings.* East Lansing: Michigan
State University, 1968.

Milner, Neal A. *The Court and Local Law Enforcement: The Impact of Miranda.*
Beverly Hills, Cal.: Sage Publications, 1971.

Mintz, Lawrence A. "Requiem for the Exclusionary Rule: Eulogy by the District of Columbia Circuit." *Howard Law Journal* 19 (1976):159-176.

Moschella, Emil P. "Probable Cause: The Officer's Shield to Suits Under the Federal Civil Rights Act." *FBI Law Enforcement Bulletin* 45 (1976):28-31.

Nagel, Stuart S. "Testing the Effects of Excluding Illegally Seized Evidence." *Wisconsin Law Review* (1965):283-310.

_____. *The Rights of the Accused in Law and Action.* Beverly Hill, Cal.: Sage Publications, 1972.

Niederhoffer, A., and Blumberg, Abraham S. *The Ambivalent Force: Perspectives on the Police.* Waltham, Mass.: Ginn and Company, 1970.

Oaks, Dallin H. "Studying the Exclusionary Rule in Search and Seizure." *University of Chicago Law Review* 37 (1970):665-757.

"On the Limitations of Empirical Evaluations of the Exclusionary Rule: A Critique of the Spiotto Research and *United States* v. *Calandra.*" *Northwestern University Law Review* 69 (1974):740-798.

Paulsen, Monrad G. "The Exclusionary Rule and Misconduct by the Police." *Journal of Criminal Law, Criminology and Police Science* 52 (1961):255-265.

Phelps, Ferinez. "When do Policemen Support the Courts?" *The Police Chief* 42 (1975):48-49.

"Police Perjury in Narcotics 'Dropsy' Cases: A New Credibility Gap." *Georgetown Law Journal* 60 (1971):507-523.

President's Commission on Law Enforcement and Administration of Justice, *Task Force Report: The Police.* Washington, D.C.: United States Government Printing Office, 1967.

Quinn, John. "Effect of Police Rulemaking on the Scope of Fourth Amendment Rights." *Journal of Urban Law* 52 (1974):25-54.

Quintana, Marsha A. "The Erosion of the Fourth Amendment Exclusionary Rule." *Howard Law Journal* 17 (1973):805-822.

Rawitscher, Jack J. "Search and Seizure: Outline Brief." *Texas Bar Journal* (1975):797-806.

Rosen, Ann. "Actionable Wrongs—Fourth Amendment Held to Be Basis of Cause for Action for Damages Against Federal Officers for Illegal Search and Seizure." *Loyola University Law Journal* 3 (1972):202-219.

Sabat, Richard J. "The Fourth Amendment: Is a Lawsuit the Answer?" *Syracuse Law Review* 23 (1972):1227-1249.

Satlin, Kenneth B. "Constitutional Law: Search and Seizure: An Alternative to the Exclusionary Rule." *JAG Journal* 26 (1972):255-261.

Sauter, Dennis C. "The Privacy Interest of the Fourth Amendment—Does *Mapp* v. *Ohio* Protect it or Pillage it? *West Virginia Law Review* 74 (1971-1972):154-162.

Schaefer, Roger C. "Patrolman Perspectives on Miranda." *Law and Social Order* (1971):81-101.

Schwartz, Herman. "Stop and Frisk (A Case Study in Judicial Control of the Police)." *Journal of Criminal Law, Criminology and Police Science.* 58 (1967):433-464.

"Search and Seizure in Illinois: Enforcement of the Constitutional Right of Privacy." *Northwestern University Law Review* 47 (1952):493-507.

Sevilla, Charles M. "The Exclusionary Rule and Police Perjury." *San Diego Law Review* 11 (1974):839-879.

Shapiro, J. Irwin. "Searches, Seizures and Lineups: Evolving Constitutional Standards Under the Warren and Burger Courts." *New York Law Forum* 20 (1974):217-252.

Silverman, David W. "Protecting the Public from *Ohio* v. *Mapp.*" *American Bar Association Journal* 51 (1965):243-245.

Simmons, Stephen J. "Criminal Law—Admissibility of Evidence: Evidence Excluded at Trial as Violative of the Fourth Amendment May Be Considered at Sentencing When It Appears the Evidence is Reliable and Not Obtained to Influence the Sentencing Judge Improperly." *University of Cincinnati Law Review* 40 (1971):172-177.

Skiba, Gary V. "The Truly Constitutional Tort." *University of Pittsburgh Law Review* 33 (1971):271-285.

Skolnick, Jerome H. *Justice Without Trial.* New York: John Wiley and Sons, 1967.

Spiotto, James E. "Search and Seizure: An Empirical Study of the Exclusionary Rule and its Alternatives." *Journal of Legal Studies* 2 (1973):243-278.

Stanley, E. John. "A Legislative Approach to the Fourth Amendment." *Nebraska Law Review* 45 (1966):148-165.

Stuckey, Gilbert B. *Evidence for the Law Enforcement Officer.* Second Edition. New York: McGraw-Hill Book Company, 1974.

Taft, Kingsley A. "Protecting the Public from *Mapp* v. *Ohio* Without Amending the Constitution." *American Bar Association Journal* 50 (1964):815-818.

Tiffany, Lawrence P. "Fourth Amendment and Police-Civilian Confrontations." *Journal of Criminal Law, Criminology and Police Science* 60 (1969):442-454.

Toensing, Victoria. "Criminal Procedure—Search and Seizure: Warrantless Searches Incident to 'Custodial Traffic Offenses' Are Included Under Search Incident to Arrest Exception to Fourth Amendment Warrant Requirement." *Journal of Urban Law* 52 (1974):177-187.

Tolin, Stefan. "The Impending Limitation of the Exclusionary Rule—Will the Supreme Court Vandalize the Constitution?" *North Carolina Central Law Journal* 5 (1973):91-97.

Tonkin, Ronald, H. "A Need to Modify the Exclusionary Rule." *Virgin Islands Bar Journal* 4 (1973):1-7.

"Tort Alternative to the Exclusionary Rule in Search and Seizure." *Journal of Criminal Law, Criminology and Police Science* 63 (1972):256-266.

Traynor, Roger J. "*Mapp* v. *Ohio* at Large in the Fifty States." *Duke Law Journal* (1962):319-343.

"Trends in Legal Commentary on the Exclusionary Rule." *Journal of Criminal Law and Criminology* 65 (1974):373-384.

Tullis, Richard and Ludlow, Linda. "Admissibility of Evidence Seized in Another Jurisdiction: Choice of Law and the Exclusionary Rule." *University of San Francisco Law Review* 10 (1975):67-91.

Turpen, Michael C. "Fundamental Principles of Search and Seizure." *Oklahoma Bar Journal Quarterly Supplement* 46 (1975):175-184.

Weinstein, Jack B. "Local Responsibility for Improvement of Search and Seizure Practices." *Rocky Mountain Law Review* 34 (1962):150-180.

White, James B. "Fourth Amendment as a Way of Talking about People: A Study of Robinson and Matlock." *The Supreme Court Review* (1974):165-232.

Williams, Parham H., Jr. "Institute on Exceptions to the Warrant Requirement Under the Fourth Amendment." *Oklahoma Law Review* 29 (1976):659-683.

Wilson, Jerry V. and Alprin, Geoffrey M. "Controlling Police Conduct: Alternatives to the Exclusionary Rule." *Law and Contemporary Problems* 36 (1971):488-499.

Wingo, Harvey. "Growing Disillusionment with the Exclusionary Rule." *Southwestern Law Journal* 25 (1971):573-593.

Wright, Charles A. "Must the Criminal Go Free if the Constable Blunders?" *Texas Law Review* 50 (1972):736-745.

Index

About the Author

J. David Hirschel received the B.A. from Cambridge University, England, and the M.A. and Ph.D. from the School of Criminal Justice at the State University of New York at Albany. He has worked in the criminal justice system in both the United States and England, and was for two years criminal justice coordinator of the Erie County, New York, Department of Anti-Rape and Sexual Assault. He is currently assistant professor of criminal justice at the University of North Carolina at Charlotte.